How To
Read Statistics

R. L. C. Butsch, Ph.D.

Late Director of Research
Rohrer, Hibler, and Replogle
Psychological Consultants to Management
Formerly Professor of Education
Marquette University

The Bruce Publishing Company
Milwaukee

Copyright, 1946
The Bruce Publishing Company
Printed in the United States of America
(Second Printing — 1949)

HOW TO READ STATISTICS

3.68

CONTENTS

HOW TO READ STATISTICS

Chapter I

INTRODUCTION

A common complaint voiced by intelligent readers in many fields is that they continually find themselves confronted with statistical procedures, or at least with statements based upon the application of such procedures. This is equally true of the teacher, the social worker, the personnel director, and the businessman who attempts to keep in touch with developments in his field, as revealed in current books and professional journals. If one wishes to know how other educators are solving the problems of the school; how other firms are selecting and retaining their employees; how other communities are meeting pressing social problems; how other industries are dealing with questions of production and distribution — he must be able to read and evaluate evidence and conclusions presented in statistical form and statistical terminology.

Since statistical techniques, and their results, are expressed in numerical form, and since many people are fearful of anything which resembles mathematics, there is a tendency among too many readers to avoid the statistical part of research reports. A large proportion of readers completely ignore the statistical treatment and merely attempt to understand the conclusions. This has been found to be true of teachers and school administrators enrolled in graduate courses. It must be even more generally true of teachers with less training; and also of busy industrial executives, or those who are concerned directly

1

with industrial relations and personnel problems. The present book is intended to aid such individuals — who do not have and do not need a thorough knowledge of the techniques of statistics — to understand materials making use of statistical procedures.

Why Bother About Statistics?

In the first place, it becomes desirable to indicate something of the purpose of statistical treatment, especially as applied to educational, social, and industrial problems.

In a word, and contrary to the opinion of many laymen, the purpose of statistics is to clarify a mass of apparently unrelated information. Statistics is a type of mathematical treatment made necessary in any field which deals with animate or living beings as distinguished from inanimate objects and forces. In the physical sciences, relationships can be expressed in the form of definite mathematical formulas. For example, a given type of gas, at a given temperature, will have a given volume which is related to the pressure to which it is subjected. This will always hold true, for all practical purposes, for that particular kind of gas, no matter where it is found. The relationship can be expressed in the form of a simple equation, and one can be certain of the results in a given situation if only his mathematics be correct. On the other hand, as soon as one deals with living beings, or groups of living beings, or the reactions or effects or products of living beings, he is not on such firm mathematical ground. One grain of wheat is not precisely like every other grain of wheat; one chicken is not precisely like every other chicken; and even more so, one child is not like every other child; one employee is not like every other employee.

The fundamental reason for the development of statistical procedures is to permit some sort of mathematical treatment of data observed in the animate group — that is, information observed concerning the measurable quantitative or qualitative characteristics, or the reactions, or effects, of any living beings. All sciences and applied arts which deal with such living subject matter have made use of statistics — for example, biology, agriculture, medicine, the social sciences, psychology, education. As a matter of fact, it is only by the application of statistics that such fields of knowledge can even aspire to become sciences. This does not mean that the application of a statistical technique automatically guarantees scientific analysis, or that the gathering of data and their statistical analysis constitute science. It only means that in many cases the discovery of scientific laws and principles will be extremely difficult, if not impossible, until a mass of seemingly unrelated data have been brought to some sort of order, and their relationships clarified by the application of statistical procedures.

The Purpose of This Book — "Why?" Rather Than "How?"

In most fields of mathematical study it has been the prevailing practice of teachers to insist that the student shall understand the derivation of all techniques, formulas, and procedures, as far as he proceeds in his study. In statistics, because of the intensely practical nature and purpose of the processes involved, there has been a tendency to emphasize, in many courses, the application rather than the derivation. In statistics, one may distinguish at least three levels of understanding. There are, first, those mathematical geniuses who discover and develop the statistical techniques required to obtain an answer to a specific type of question. Second, there are those who, with an extensive mathematical background, are able to follow the mathematical reasoning of the first group, and understand fully the derivation and use of the techniques. A third, and much larger group, comprises those who have been trained in the ordinary courses in educational, social, and business statistics to carry out a particular statistical procedure, to apply a particular formula, and to interpret — often in a purely mechanical fashion — the results so obtained.

Beyond these three groups, it appears that there are a large number of teachers, social workers, personnel directors, and industrial executives, who through lack of opportunity or inclination have failed to acquire the minimum of statistical techniques implied for the third group. Many of these, however, should be able to read the articles employing statistical procedures, and should, at least, be able to understand the purpose and the results of the techniques employed. It is for the sake of this large group that the present discussion will attempt to explain something of the purposes and aims of the various statistical techniques and of the application of statistics to industrial, social, and educational problems. The emphasis will be upon the interpretation of statistical treatment and statistical terminology, without a complete explanation of the procedures or techniques. In other words, the attempt will be made to enable the reader to become an intelligent "consumer" of statistics, in so far as that can be done without asking him to become acquainted with the mathematics involved in carrying out statistical computation. The emphasis will be on "Why is it done?" and "What does it mean?" rather than on "How is it obtained?"

Chapter II

THE FREQUENCY DISTRIBUTION

Light on a Jumble of Figures

One of the simplest operations related to statistical interpretation — and usually among the first to be applied, especially if a large amount of information has been gathered
— has as its purpose discovering and making clear the
nature of the distribution of the items.

Suppose, for example, that one is conducting a survey of
a community in order to determine the number of children
in each family. Such a problem might arise in a general
social survey, or it might also be found in a school survey
where the purpose is to determine present and future school
needs. The investigator, in covering a small section of the
community, might find that in the houses, taken in order
as he came to them, the following numbers of children were
reported:

1	1	2	0	1	3	5	1	1	2
4	3	1	1	0	0	2	5	2	3
6	7	2	1	1	3	2	2	1	0
4	2	0	4	0	6	0	5	2	1

Merely glancing at this list, or even examining it in some
detail, gives nothing but a confused idea to the effect that
there are many small families, and that a family of more
than five children is very rare. The entire list might be

put in order, from the smallest to the largest, resulting in the following array:

```
0  0  0  0  0  0  0  1  1  1
1  1  1  1  1  1  1  1  2  2
2  2  2  2  2  2  2  3  3  3
3  4  4  4  5  5  5  6  6  7
```

Such an arrangement becomes much more enlightening, but still requires more space for a report than is necessary. A glance at the rearranged list immediately suggests that it would be satisfactory merely to note how many families there are, each reporting a given number of children. When this procedure is adopted, the data appear as follows:

No. of Children	No. of Families	
7	1	7.
6	2	12
5	3	15.
4	3	12
3	4	12
2	9	18.
1	11	11.
0	7	
Total	40	87

$$\bar{x} = 2.19$$

This is an example of a very simple type of *frequency distribution;* or a distribution showing the frequency of occurrence of cases of individuals having a given trait in some measurable degree (in this case, of families with a certain number of children).

Frequency Distribution With Class Intervals Larger Than One Unit

In many cases it will not be possible or desirable to indicate the frequency of occurrence of each specific score or number. This will be true especially where the spread from the smallest to the largest recorded item of information is much greater than in the example just given. Suppose, for instance, that the school authorities in a given community are interested in knowing something about the variation in size of classes in the high school. Taking classes at random, or period by period, or teacher by teacher, might result in a list which started out as follows:

22,	15,	29,	21,	12,	35,	31,	28,	27,	19
24,	14,	10,	32,	33,	28,	29,	18,	17,	31
30,	29,	22,	8,	27,	13,	15,	29,	33,	34
15,	7,	12,	24,	26,	36,	34,	30,	26,	9

A casual inspection of this list is even more confusing than an examination of the first example; the only result would be a confused idea to the effect that there are some small, some moderate-sized, and some large classes. In this case, again, the items in the list might be put in order from the smallest to the largest, an operation which would not be very complicated for the number of classes here involved. But, if information were obtained for many more teachers and classes, the difficulty of putting the numbers in order would increase, and the usefulness of the resulting distribution would decrease.

In such a case, it is customary to arrange the items of information in a frequency distribution, but in this instance it would be very unsatisfactory to attempt to indicate exactly how many classes there are of every possible size, from the smallest, with 7 pupils, to the largest, with 35. For one thing, there would be many possible class sizes for which there would be no instances at all, and there would be at best only a few classes of any particular size. Therefore, the data are arranged in groups of convenient size, and the number of cases, or classes, within each group is indicated. For example, if the data listed above were distributed by groups of 10 pupils, they would look as follows:

No. of Pupils	No. of Classes
30–39	11
20–29	15 *mode*
10–19	11
0– 9	3
Total	40

Even such a gross distribution as this throws some light on the situation. Thus, it is clear that there are very few classes of less than 10 pupils; and that there are more classes of from 20 to 29 pupils than are found elsewhere in the table. It might be considered helpful to make a distribution with small ranges in the groups of class intervals — for example, if only those classes with 5 to 9 pupils were grouped together, and those with 10 to 14 pupils, etc., the table would appear as follows:

No. of Pupils	No. of Classes
35–39	2
30–34	9
25–29	10 *Mode*
20–24	5 *MEDIAN*
15–19	6
10–14	5
5– 9	3
Total	40

This grouping has the advantage of making clear that there are only 2 classes of over 35 pupils; that there are none with less than 5; and that the most common sizes of class are those numbering between 25 and 34 pupils.

One disadvantage of a frequency distribution (or a tabulation showing the grouping of the data, as above) is that the identity of individual cases is lost. Thus, of the 10 classes with enrollments of from 25 to 29 pupils, it is not clear from the table how many have 29, how many 28, etc.

On the other hand, in most instances, a picture of the general grouping is more important than a knowledge of each individual case.

Telling the Story in a Picture

An advantage of the frequency distribution, or table grouping the data into various classifications, is that it

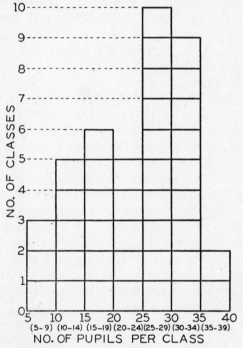

Figure 1. A typical graph of a frequency distribution.

makes possible a graphical representation of the information. For instance, a graph of the last table given above, with class intervals of 5, is shown in Figure 1. In this figure, each square represents one class. Thus, above the space indicated as 5–9 pupils per class, there are 3 squares, which is interpreted as meaning that there are 3 classes found in this size range. Above the space indicated as 25–29, there are 10 squares, representing 10 classes of that size, etc.

Some readers can understand more readily if they see a picture such as shown in this graph. Others can grasp the situation more quickly by looking at a frequency distribution, as in the table given above. Others may more readily comprehend by reading the discussion, such as follows the table. A good piece of statistical research, intended for general reading, will provide the information in all these forms, in the hope that one or more may be intelligible to each individual who wishes to read and understand it.

The only point which the casual reader of statistical material needs to keep in mind in connection with the tabular presentation of data is that this device is used to bring out certain relationships which would not be obvious in the ungrouped data. It is necessary whenever a large number of items of information have been obtained because the reader — or the writer, for that matter — could not keep in mind the essential facts about each item. For instance, it is difficult to recognize and think about, individually, even the 40 items of information given above, until they are put in tabular form. And the more data or cases (in this instance, classes) the more important does this type of assistance to one's thinking become.

Chapter III

MEASURES OF CENTRAL TENDENCY

One of the most common questions asked about a group of data is, "What is the average?" of the group. Another very common question is, "How does this group compare with some other group?" For example, one might ask, "What is the average size of class in this high school?" And also, "How does the size of class in our school compare with that in other cities?" Or, "What is the average score made by this fifth grade in School A on a certain standardized test in arithmetic?" And, "How does this fifth grade compare with the fifth grade in School B?" It will be the purpose of this chapter to show how these questions are answered.

The Frequency Distribution Alone Is Not Satisfactory

While the arrangement of the data into groups, as done in a frequency distribution or table, aids materially in clarifying the information, such a table becomes somewhat cumbersome for certain purposes, such as those just suggested. For example, as indicated above, the school board might be interested in knowing the distribution of sizes of classes not only for the local high school, but also for other communities of the same type or size. While a complete comparison would involve the examination of the tables, for the various schools, such examination might give in one sense more, and in another sense less, information than was desired. In other words, it very often is adequate,

11

$$\sigma = \sqrt{\frac{\Sigma x^2}{N}}$$

and frequently is more revealing, if one single measure or number can be used to express or stand for a complete distribution or complete set of data. In common language, it is sometimes more significant to know, for example, the "average" size of class in each school involved in the comparison.

Two Measures of "Average," or Central Tendency

When one hears about averages for the first time in his elementary school experience, he learns that if he adds together, say, 10 numbers which represent his grade in spelling for 10 days, and then divides this total by 10, his result will be the "average" grade in spelling for those 10 days. The statistician uses the word average in a somewhat more general sense than this common interpretation. He applies it to all measures of what he terms *central tendency*. One of these measures of central tendency which he calls the *mean* or *arithmetic mean* is nothing more or less than the "average" of one's elementary school experience. Another term, which is used with considerable frequency in educational statistics, is called the *median*. The difference between these two measures can perhaps be made clear by noting their definitions, and by observing some examples.

The arithmetic mean, or common average, is defined simply as the sum of all of the scores divided by the number of scores. For example, if five boys have, respectively, 25, 18, 15, 12, and 10 marbles, the mean or "average" number of marbles per boy will be the total number, or 80, divided among the five boys; or 16 marbles. The median is sometimes defined loosely as "the middle measure" (of those involved); but more precisely as "that point on the scale above which and below which an equal number of cases lie." Using the less precise definition, the median number of marbles per boy in the example just given would

$$M = \frac{\Sigma X}{N}$$

be 15, since two boys have more and two boys have less than 15 marbles. Of course, for such small numbers and so few cases (boys) the computation or determination of the mean and median will be very simple. However, as more and more cases are added, and especially if the information is put into the form of a frequency distribution (showing the number of individuals in each group — those having from 10 to 20 marbles, from 20 to 30 marbles, etc.), other procedures are used to obtain the mean and the median. There is no need to go into the method of computation here, as that is not the purpose of this discussion.

The Difference Between the Mean and the Median

The principal difference between the mean and the median (which is implied in the definitions given) is that the former is influenced by the exact size of each individual score or measure, while the latter takes into account only the general relative size or position in the distribution. The difference may be made more clear by a simple example. Suppose that, in the inquiry by the school board into the number of pupils per class which was indicated above, it is found that the classes in one department are as follows:

32, 28, 26, 25, 24, 23, 22, 21, 19, 19, 16

For these eleven classes the total number of pupils is 253, and the mean number per class (average, in ordinary usage) is 23 (253 divided by 11). Since the numbers above are arranged in order from the largest to the smallest, the sixth class, counting from either top or bottom, satisfies one of the definitions of the median — in other words, it is the middle measure. For this list of eleven classes, therefore, the mean and median coincide at 23.

The next group of eleven classes, for the next department, is found to be as follows:

34, 33, 33, 32, 29, 23, 22, 22, 21, 20, 19

For this list, the total number of pupils involved is 286, and the mean size of class is found to be 26. However, in counting down, or up, to the sixth or middle case, it is found that the median for this group is ~~also~~ 23. In other words, in each department, half of the classes have more than 23 pupils, and half have less than 23. But the mean (or common average) number of pupils per class is 23 in the first department and 26 in the second. This difference is caused by the fact that in the second group, of those classes which are above the median of 23, one has 29 pupils and the others all have more than 30, while in the first group, on the other hand, three of the classes are close to 23, and only one has over 30 pupils. The classes below the median of 23 are also seen to be larger in the second group than in the first. This illustrates how the mean is influenced by the actual value of the score, while the median is influenced only by the position of the score above or below the central measure.

The Difference Between Mean and Median Illustrated by Frequency Distributions

This difference between the mean and median will be illustrated further by an examination of the two distributions given in Table 1. It will be observed that in both classes, 2 pupils had scores on the test which were between 90 and 99; 5 had scores between 80 and 89; 16 between 70 and 79; 24 between 60 and 69; and 23 between 50 and 59. Since more than half of the 100 cases are included in these five groups or class intervals, the median — the point above which and below which half of the cases fall — will be the same for each distribution, namely 58.3. (The exact method by which this figure is obtained is not explained here, since no attempt is being made to teach computational technique. Suffice it to say that the method used can be shown to be derived by logical processes from the simple procedure used in the preceding examples.) On the other

TABLE I

Comparison of Mean and Median

Scores on Test	Number of Pupils Obtaining a Score Within the Group or Class Interval Indicated	
	Class A	Class B
90–99	2	2
80–89	5	5
70–79	16	16
60–69	24	24
50–59	23	23
40–49	17	8
30–39	8	2
20–29	3	1
10–19	1	2
0– 9	1	17
Total	100	100
Mean	57.4	52.1
Median	58.3	58.3

hand, the mean will be affected by the extreme irregularity of the second class — by the fact that there are 17 pupils who had scores from 0 to 9. The mean of the first distribution is about the same as the median, namely, 57.4. For the second distribution, however, the mean is found to be 52.1. (Again the exact procedure is not indicated — but is based on the simple definition of the mean used in the example above.) The effect of extreme cases on this measure of central tendency is made clear by this rather unusual distribution.

A Graphical Illustration of the Difference Between Mean and Median

The difference between median and mean can also be explained by graphical representation of the distribution for these two classes as shown in Figure 2. It will be noted

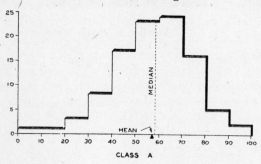

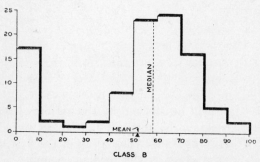

Figure 2. Median and mean graphically compared.

that since the median is merely that point on the scale above which and below which an equal number of cases lie, a line can be drawn through the graph at the point of the median; half of the cases will then fall on either side of this line. It will be observed that this line is at the same point for the two distributions.

Now assume that these graphical figures have thickness, and therefore weight. The mean, in each case, is that point or fulcrum upon which the figure could be balanced. Just as on a teeter-totter a small child at a distance from the center will balance a much larger child nearer the center on the other side, so the extreme cases overbalance many more cases much closer to the center. In other words, the further a case is from the center of the distribution, the more effect it will have on the mean. It is therefore said that the mean is influenced by, and reflects accurately, the exact size of every measure in the distribution; while the median merely indicates that point on either side of which half the cases fall — the distances of the cases from the point having no effect on this measure of central tendency.

The Measure of Central Tendency to Be Used Depends Upon Nature and Purpose of Study

While other measures of central tendency are found occasionally, these two, median and mean, will enable one to read most articles in educational and social research, in so far as central tendency is concerned. Which measure is more satisfactory depends largely on the nature of the data, as well as the type of information which one wishes to obtain. For example, a study of the length of service of teachers brought out the following conclusions: The mean period of service, which is affected by the proportionately small number of teachers with 30 or more years of experience, was found to be over 8 years. On the other hand, since there were many teachers who served only 1 or 2 years, the median was found to be about 4.5 years. Both items of information are, of course, of significance. It is important to know that the average or mean length of time that teachers remained in service at the time of the study was something over 8 years, since that number would have some relationship to the rate at which the total groups would have to be replaced by new teachers. On the other hand, it is also important to know that half of the teachers involved served less than 4½ years. Thus, in some types of problems, one measure is preferred; in some, the other; and in many cases both the median and the mean are valuable for the aid they give in interpretation.

Chapter IV

MEASURES OF DISPERSION

While a knowledge of the central tendency of a distribution is important, for many purposes other information will also be essential. Equally necessary is information about the nature of a distribution — whether the cases or individual scores are grouped closely about the mean or median, or are widely scattered or dispersed. For example, in a given city the school board and the superintendent have been interested in examining the results of some standardized tests given to the pupils in their schools. They find that the average score on the arithmetic test made by the fifth grade in School A is 68. Looking further, they find that the average made by the fifth grade of School B is also 68. They might then hastily conclude that the two classes were similar; that they were of the same level of ability, or that the teachers were equally effective, or both.

Why the Average Alone May Mislead

But a closer examination of the distributed scores for the two classes reveals certain interesting but disquieting information. It is found that in School A the fifth graders had scores which ranged from 58 to 78, and that most of them earned between 66 and 70 in the test. In School B, however, it is discovered that about a third of the class had scores around 30, another third had scores over 95, and only three pupils fell in the range between 60 and 80. Obviously, the members of the first class were all very similar in their knowledge of arithmetic. On the other hand, a large number of those in the second class do not reveal such knowledge as would justify their being promoted, while another group of approximately the same size are decidedly above the level to be expected. The pupils in School A may have been more alike to begin with, or the teacher may have striven to see that all acquired the learnings expected. The pupils in School B may not have belonged together at all, or the teacher may have concentrated her attention on the responsive individuals, and neglected the others. At any rate, the two classes cannot now be given the same treatment, even though the average grade is the same in each case. Such a situation (while it may be somewhat exaggerated) indicates the necessity of additional analysis of the data.

As another illustration, the superintendent's report might show that the average number of pupils per teacher in two schools was exactly the same, say 25. A superficial examination would suggest that the work was being equally divided among the teachers. But a closer inspection might reveal that in the first school nearly all classes had from 23 to 28 pupils, with only a few above 30, or below 20; while in the second school most of the classes were above 30 or below 20, and only a few near the average.

How the Amount of Scattering Is Measured

These two examples illustrate the need for some measure which will describe the way in which data are grouped about the mean or other average: whether they cluster closely, or are widely dispersed. To be sure, if the entire frequency tabulation is furnished, it is possible to examine it and come to some conclusion regarding the degree of the dispersion, or scattering. However, in this case also the statistician would like to describe the condition with a single number in order to make it easier to draw conclusions about the distribution, and especially to compare it with other similar distributions. For this purpose several *measures of dispersion* have been devised. These are also variously known as measures of variation, of variability, of spread, etc. The one which is used most frequently in educational research is called the *standard deviation,* and is also indicated by the Greek letter σ, or sometimes is written *sigma.* Other measures used for this same purpose are known as the *quartile deviation,* and the *mean deviation* or *average deviation.*

Although it is not the intent of this discussion to describe in detail the exact procedure for computing the various statistical measures which are presented, it is still necessary, in the case of measures of dispersion, to indicate briefly the nature of the process of computation. These measures are merely arbitrary, and are best defined by means of the formula or description of the method of deriving them. However, the important point here is to know in a general way what sort of measure is signified.

What the Quartile Deviation Means

The *quartile deviation,* frequently expressed by the symbol "Q," is a measure obtained by counting, as is the median. This measure of dispersion depends upon the location of two points, known as the first quartile and the third quartile. Just as the median is defined as "that point on the scale above which and below which one-half of the measures lie," so the first quartile, or "Q_1," may be defined as that point below which one-fourth, and above which three-fourths of the cases are found. Similarly, the third quartile, or "Q_3," is the point below which three-fourths, and above which one-fourth, of the cases are located. Q, or the *quartile deviation,* or, more precisely but also more cumbersomely, *the semi-inter-quartile range,* is one-half the distance between Q_1 and Q_3.

In other words, Q is a measure in terms of the scale on which the scores are recorded, which is half the distance, on the base line of a graph, of the segment of the distribution which includes the middle half of the cases. It is to be observed that unless the middle half of the distribution is symmetrical about the median — that is to say, unless just as many cases lie at the same distance within each segment above and below the median — Q is not the distance from the median to either Q_1 or Q_3. It is, however, in every case, one-half the distance between Q_1 and Q_3, even when these points lie at unequal distances above and below the median.

Sometimes the dispersion or variation is measured by the entire inter-quartile range, or the distance between Q_1 and Q_3. The complete range, from the lowest score to the highest, is also sometimes used as a rough measure of dispersion. However, of these counting measures, Q is the most common.

In order to see the significance of Q, let us consider, for example, the following list of forty scores:

99	88	85	80
98	88	85	79
96	87	85	79
94	87	85	78
93	87	85	77
92	87	84	75
92	86	84	74
91	86	84	73
91	86	83	70
90	86	82	68

The median is at the point 85.5, since half of the cases fall above that score, and half below. Similarly, the first quartile, Q_1, is at the point 81, since one-fourth of the scores are less than 81, and three-fourths are above 81.

The third quartile, Q_3, is found to be 89, since one-fourth of the scores fall above, and three-fourths fall below that point. The total *inter-quartile range,* or the total distance between the first and third quartiles, is therefore 89 minus 81, or 8 points. The *semi-inter-quartile range,* or half that distance — which is, by definition, Q — is, therefore, one-half of 8, or 4. This illustrates the simple definition of Q which may be used when the actual scores are arranged in order. When the scores are put in a frequency distribution, this simple method, of course, will not apply.

Other Measures of Dispersion

The other measures of dispersion, the *mean deviation* and the *standard deviation,* take into account the exact distance of each case from the measure of central tendency. The nature of these measures is shown by the following example, for which the data are given in Table II. It is assumed that these are the scores obtained by nine pupils on a test. It will be observed that for the nine numbers given, the mean is 60. The deviations of the scores from this mean, given in the next column of the table, are: 12, 9, 6, 3, 0, −3, −6, −9, −12. Obviously, if these numbers are added algebraically (that is, taking account of the positive and negative signs), the sum will be zero, as each positive deviation is balanced by an equal negative deviation. There are two ways in which the signs can be kept from canceling each other. One is to add the numbers in the column headed "Deviations From Mean," paying no attention to the plus and minus signs. The sum, or total deviation, in this case is 60; the *average deviation* or *mean deviation* would thus be 60 divided by 9 (the number of cases), or 6.67.

The other procedure which eliminates the effects of differences in sign, is to square each deviation, as is done in the next column of Table II. The sum of these "squared

TABLE II

Mean Deviation and Standard Deviation

Scores on Test Made by Individual Pupils	Deviations From Mean	Squares of Deviations
72	12	144
69	9	81
66	6	36
63	3	9
(Mean) 60	0	0
57	− 3	9
54	− 6	36
51	− 9	81
48	−12	144

Total   540
Mean   60 (M)

Algebraic Total................. 0
Total (Ignoring signs)............ 60

Mean Deviation................. 6.67 (M.D.)
  Sum of Squared Deviations.........540
  Mean of Squared Deviations......... 60
  Square Root of the Mean.......... 7.746 (σ)

deviations" is found to be 540. Since there are 9 cases, the average of the "squared deviation" is 540 divided by 9, or 60. Since the deviations were squared, it is only natural to take the square root of this average in order to bring the result back to the same type of number as the original data. The square root of 60 is found to be 7.746; and this number is known as the *standard deviation,* or *sigma.* A descriptive but clumsy definition for this measure is the *root mean square of the deviations;* in other words, the deviations from the mean are squared, the squares are added, and the sum is divided by the number of cases to give the mean square of the deviations; then the square root of this mean square is extracted. For larger numbers of cases, and for data grouped in a frequency distribution, the computation of both mean deviation and standard deviation becomes more complicated, and there is no need to describe the procedure at this time.

Interpretation of Measures of Dispersion

Table III will show the effect of variations in the distribution on the various measures of dispersion. It is assumed that the school board has finally brought together informa-

TABLE III

Comparison of the Mean and Measures of Dispersion

No. of Pupils Per Class	No. of Classes Having No. of Pupils Falling Within the Groups Indicated		
	School A	School B	School C
33–35	1	10	19
30–32	5	11	18
27–29	12	12	6
24–26	18	11	4
21–25	26	12	2
18–20	17	10	5
15–17	13	9	9
12–14	7	13	18
9–11	1	12	19
Total	100	100	100
Mean	22.39	22.39	22.39
Standard Deviation	4.97	7.78	9.49
Quartile Deviation	3.55	7.00	9.50
Mean Deviation	3.92	6.72	8.97

tion on the size of classes in three high schools, and the data are shown in Table III for 100 classes in each school. In School A, for example, there is only 1 class of 33 to 35 pupils; 26, of 21 to 23 pupils; and only 1 of 9 to 11 pupils. In School B, there are 10 classes out of the 100 of 33 to 35 pupils, and in School C, 19 classes fall in this group. When the measures of central tendency are computed, it is found that the mean (or ordinary average) for each school is exactly the same, namely, 22.39 pupils per class. Obviously, however, the conditions are not the same in the three schools. An examination of the column for School A indicates that most of the classes are near the average in size, with only a few extremely large or small classes. The next column, for School B, makes it clear that in that school there are about the same number of classes in each size group indicated — nearly as many large classes and small classes as average-sized classes. In the third column, for School C, it is revealed that most of the classes are either large — consisting of 30 or more pupils — or small — having less than 15 pupils. Very few are near the average in size.

When the complete distributions are presented these comparisons can be made directly, although in the general terms just used in the preceding paragraph. However, the statistician would like to be able to express these conditions in more compact form, and especially to be able to indicate the nature of these distributions without actually showing them. It is for this purpose, among others, that measures of dispersion are used. In the lower part of Table III are shown the three measures of dispersion described above, for each of the three schools. While these figures differ among themselves, they have this in common — they do differentiate between the three types of distributions shown. Thus, for School A, where the classes are in the main near the average in size, the quartile deviation, the mean deviation, and the standard deviation are all small. For School B, where there are nearly an equal number of large, average, and small classes, all three measures of dispersion are considerably larger. For School C, in which most classes are either very large or very small, the three measures of dispersion are still larger.

A Brief Method of Describing the Distributions

In other words, the statistician might have merely reported means and standard deviations for the three schools, as follows:

	Mean	Standard Deviation
School A	22.39	4.97
School B	22.39	7.78
School C	22.39	9.49

Any reader who understands statistical terminology would immediately recognize that while the means were the same, the distributions were entirely different in the three schools. Without seeing the distributions of Table III at all, such a reader would conclude that the classes were more nearly of similar size in School A, because it has the smallest standard deviation. He would also recognize that there were probably many very large and many very small classes in School C, since the standard deviation for this school is the largest of the three. He would also decide that the distribution for School B fell somewhat between these two extremes, since its standard deviation is between the other two. The same conclusion would be reached, in this case, if the dispersions had been reported in terms of the quartile deviation, or of the mean deviation.

In other words, for distributions of data of the same type, and in which the central tendencies are fairly similar, a small measure of dispersion (a small Q, a small σ, or a small M.D.) will indicate a distribution concentrated rather closely about the central tendency (M. or Md). And the larger the measure of dispersion, the greater is the scattering, or dispersion, of the data away from this central tendency. It should be noted, however, that such a conclusion is justified only under the conditions mentioned, namely, for data of the same type, with reasonably similar central tendencies or averages.

Chapter V

GRAPHICAL REPRESENTATION

Simple Comparison of Differences in Magnitude

One of the most important tools of the statistician in his attempt to make clear the meaning of data is the graph. Any information which can be represented by a table can also be shown by means of a graph. The principal advantage of a graph is that it is more concrete than a table; its principal disadvantage is that it does not permit such fine distinctions as the table of data. In many instances, however, it is more important that the reader see clearly the contrast between two or more quantities, or recognize the trend of the information, than that he know precisely, to the last decimal place, how large a particular difference may be.

The first, and simplest, type of graph is that which compares two quantities. For instance, the superintendent's report to the school board shows that the enrollment in School A is 320 pupils, while that in School B is 390 pupils. Even in such a simple comparison as that, the statistician must make a choice between several graphical methods of representing the data. In general, there are four different methods of indicating quantity graphically: by length, by area, by volume, and by angle. In this simple case which has been chosen for purposes of illustration, the two items of information may be shown in each of these ways.

Bar Graphs Are Commonest

The most common method of representing these data is shown in Figure 3-*A*. In this case, the number of pupils in each school is represented by the length of a horizontal bar. It should be noted that the length of the two bars must

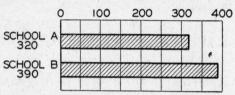

Figure 3-*A*. A common horizontal bar graph.

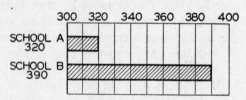

Figure 3-*B*. Incorrect — the bars start at 300 instead of 0.

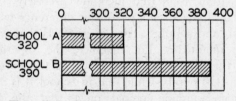

Figure 3-*C*. Correct — breaks show elimination of part of the graph.

be proportionate to the numbers represented — in other words, they must both start at a common line, which is zero on the scale. Sometimes through ignorance, and sometimes with intent to mislead, the maker of a graph may start at a point which is not zero, as shown in the incorrect graph, Figure 3-*B*. In this case, the point 300 has been taken as the starting point. The result is that the unwary reader, failing to note the 300 point on the scale, may interpret the figure as indicating that School B is four and one-half times as large of School A. Whenever, for some good reason, some point other than zero on the scale is chosen for the beginning of the graph, the careful writer will so indicate by making a break in both the scale and the bars themselves, as shown in Figure 3-*C*. Another common and equally correct method of representing the same two items of information is the use of perpendicular bars, as shown in Figure 3-*D*. In this case again, the figure may be misleading if some point other than zero is taken as the starting point, as in Figure 3-*E*. The discrepancy may be avoided, as in the case of the horizontal bars, by an indication that part

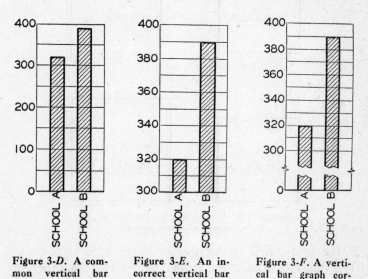

Figure 3-*D*. A common vertical bar graph.

Figure 3-*E*. An incorrect vertical bar graph.

Figure 3-*F*. A vertical bar graph correctly broken.

of the scale has been eliminated from the graph, as in
Figure 3-*F*.

Differences in Area

The same items of information may be represented, if it
seems desirable, by differences in area. However, in this
case both the writer and the reader must be on their guard
so that incorrect interpretation will not result. The only
correct procedure is to make the areas themselves proportional to the quantities. This requisite, however, leads to
difficulties in reading the graph. A correct picture of these
two quantities, represented by areas, is shown in Figure
4-*A*. In this case, the sides of the squares are proportional

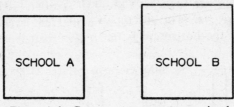

Figure 4-*A*. Correct — areas are proportional
to quantities.

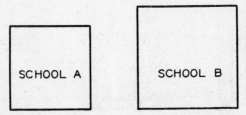

Figure 4-*B*. Incorrect — heights are proportional to quantities.

to the square root of the number of pupils in each school.
The difficulty is that the reader must make allowance for
this fact, and must compare areas, and not heights. An

incorrect representation of these same data is shown in Figure 4-*B*. In this case, the heights of the squares are made proportional to the number of pupils. The reader is spared the necessity of keeping in mind the square root of the number of pupils, but unless this variation in usage is made perfectly clear in the title of the graph, a misconception is very likely to result.

Cubes for Volumetric Graphs

Quantities may also be compared by graphs representing differences in volumes, but this procedure is still more likely to result in misinterpretation. In Figure 5-*A* are shown two cubes whose volumes are proportional to the number of pupils in the two schools. Unless the reader is very much on his guard, he is likely to conclude that the difference between the two numbers is much less than it actually is. One is just not accustomed to interpreting differences in volume as readily as differences in length. If the difference

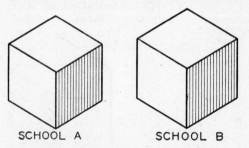

SCHOOL A   SCHOOL B

Figure 5-*A*. Small differences in magnitude are not easily detected in volumetric graphs.

between the two magnitudes compared is small in comparison to their total size, figures which are difficult to interpret, as in Figure 5-*A*, result. If the difference is large in comparison to their total size, it may be more readily distinguished, as in Figure 5-*B*. In this case, the magnitudes compared are 20 and 90. The difference between them is the same as the difference between 320 and 390; but the contrast is much more obvious in Figure 5-*B* than in 5-*A*.

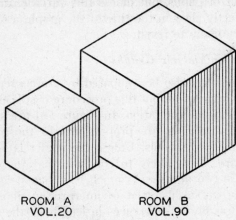

ROOM A   ROOM B
VOL.20   VOL.90

Figure 5-*B*. Differences in magnitude must be large for contrast.

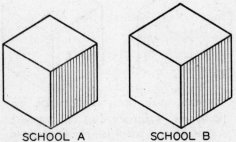

SCHOOL A   SCHOOL B

Figure 5-*C*. Incorrect — areas of the front surfaces are proportional to quantities.

In addition, two incorrect forms may result from the attempt to use volumes for such a representation. In Figure 5-*C* the areas of the fronts of the cubes have been made proportional to the two quantities. This graph is, perhaps, easier to interpret, but may lead to erroneous conclusions unless the nature of the change has been made perfectly clear. In Figure 5-*D* the sides of the cubes have been made proportional to the number of pupils in each school. This graph involves a mere comparison of lengths, but there is no clear reason why volumes should be used at all if comparisons of lengths is desired.

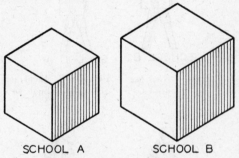

SCHOOL A   SCHOOL B

Figure 5-*D*. Incorrect — sides are proportional to quantities.

Pictures Make Graphs Interesting

Sometimes for the sake of added clarity, pictorial graphs are used. For example, one might draw a picture of a school child to represent the enrollment in each school. If the picture is merely a flat outline, the rules of representing quantities by areas must be followed. Figure 6-*A* shows a correct graph in which the *areas* of the two figures are proportional to the number of pupils in the two schools. Frequently, however, the *heights* of the figures may be made proportional to the quantities, resulting in possible misinterpretation. This incorrect procedure is shown in Figure 6-*B*. If the figures are shown in solid form, even more difficulty may result. A correct representation would involve the use of volume to indicate the number of cases in each figure, as shown in Figure 6-C. Incorrect representations would be made if either the area or the height were made proportional to the quantities to be indicated.

SCHOOL A   SCHOOL B   SCHOOL A   SCHOOL B

Figure 6-*A*. Correct — areas are proportional to quantities.   Figure 6-*B*. Incorrect — heights are proportional to quantities.

SCHOOL A   SCHOOL B

Figure 6-*C*. Correct — volume is proportional to quantities.

Recently the values of pictorial representation and the exactness of linear graphs have been combined in many educational writings by the type of graph shown in Figure 7. In this case, the figure of a child is drawn to indicate that the data refer to enrollments of children. However, the figures are all drawn exactly the same size, and each figure is made to indicate a given number. In this case, each figure represents fifty children. This type of graph is valuable in that it emphasizes the pictorial nature of the representation;

and it also permits a general comparison of quantity. However, one does not usually make quite such a fine distinc-

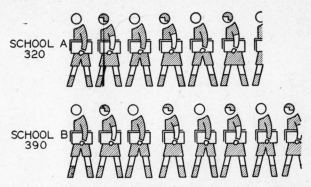

SCHOOL A
320

SCHOOL B
390

Figure 7. A combination of pictorial representation and the linear graph.

tion in the number of cases as he might with a simple line graph. This type serves admirably when the graph maker has to give the reader only a general idea of the difference between magnitudes.

The Familiar Pie Graph

Only one other method of comparing quantities graphically remains; namely, interpretation of angles. This method is used almost entirely in cases in which the quantities to be compared make up a whole. For example, in the illustration which we have been using, if it is assumed that these are the only two elementary schools in a particular system, the information might well be represented as in Figure 8-*A*. In this case, a circle has been drawn, and by angular measure the two quantities have been represented. This has often been referred to as the "pie" graph, because of its resemblance to a pie which has been cut. The important point to be remembered here is that the angle at the center of the circle shows what proportion of the total is represented by the enrollment in each school. As a matter of fact, in reading such a graph, one is usually swayed in his interpretation by the relative sizes of the two sectors of the circle. How-

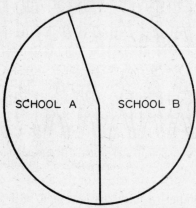

Figure 8-*A*. A circle, or pie, graph.

ever, this is not important, since the areas cut off will be exactly proportional to the angles at the center. The size of the circle which is used is of no importance — any size which conveniently fits the space allotted to the graph may be chosen.

Figure 8-*B*. The bar graph used to compare parts of a whole.

This same type of data — representing the parts of a whole — may also be shown by a slight variation in the bar graph, as in Figure 8-*B*. In this case, the entire length of the bar represents all of the cases. The length of each section of the bar, usually shaded differently, represents the proportion of the whole which is found in each part — in this case, in each school.

General Rules for the Simple Comparison of Differences in Magnitude

Of the various graphical forms which have been shown in the figures, to represent the simple data used for this illustration, certain types are obviously more satisfactory. Good usage among statisticians — supported by experimental evidence — tends in the following direction: Quantities may usually be represented more satisfactorily by bars, each starting from the zero point. The horizontal bar seems to have some advantage over the vertical bar in that more information in numerical form may be incorporated in the figure itself. The use of areas or volumes for representing quantities leads to serious danger of misinterpretation. When general comparison is sufficient, graphs consisting of lines of pictures are very effective. When quantities to be compared are the component parts of a whole, the use of a circle — the so-called "pie" graph — with sectors cut off by angles proportional to the quantities, may often be more satisfactory than any other procedure.

So far only very simple illustrations have been used which involve the comparison of just two quantities. Naturally, the methods described above are also applicable to the comparison of more than two quantities — just where the limit of useful representation may lie is still a matter of some dispute. There also remains for consideration the use of graphs to represent data which vary according to some point of reference, such as time. These further applications of the graphical method will be considered next.

Chapter VI

MORE COMPLEX FORMS OF GRAPHS

The previous chapter was limited to the simple case of the comparison of two magnitudes, in order to make clear the various types of figures which may be used for that purpose. In actual practice, of course, such simple numbers as were used would hardly need to be presented graphically; the comparison would be clear from the mere statement of the quantities themselves. However, the principles of effective representation illustrated are equally valid when applied to more complicated sets of data. The present chapter will extend these principles to more complex situations.

Simple Comparison of More Than Two Magnitudes

Suppose, for example, that the superintendent, in his report to the board, wishes to represent the enrollment by grade in one particular school. His data might be those of the column headed "School A" in Table IV. In this case the horizontal bar graph shown in Figure 10 would probably be the most satisfactory form to employ. The advantage of the horizontal over the vertical, of course, is that the data themselves may be entered at the side of the bars in the figure. If this is not desirable, the vertical bar graph is equally satisfactory. These same data may, of course, be represented by means of a circle, or "pie," graph. In this case, the magnitudes are equal to the angles at the center of the circle. This form is shown in Figure 9.

TABLE IV

Enrollments in Each Grade in Each of the Five Schools
of a Particular Community

Grade	School A	School B	School C	School D	School E
1	68	80	72	97	92
2	58	69	58	81	88
3	57	64	52	80	85
4	60	62	64	74	87
5	59	60	58	76	84
6	62	65	60	82	80
7	56	68	60	85	80
8	60	72	66	80	79
Total	480	540	490	655	675

An extension of this form of comparison is that in which
the data for two schools are to be compared. The data given
in the columns headed "School B" and "School C" in Table
IV indicate the number of pupils in each grade of two

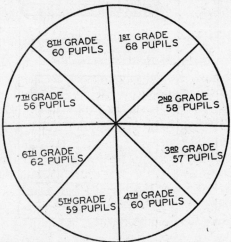

Figure 9. A circle graph comparing class
sizes of School A given in Table IV.

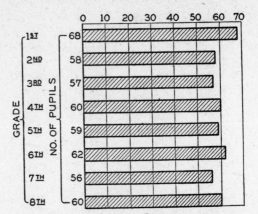

Figure 10. A bar graph comparing class sizes
of School A given in Table IV.

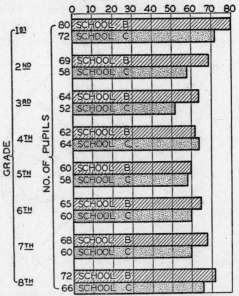

Figure 11. A bar graph comparing class sizes
of Schools B and C given in Table IV.

schools in the same community. The quantities given in the table are also represented by Figure 11. In this case, it should be observed that it is necessary to distinguish, by crosshatching or otherwise, between the bars which stand

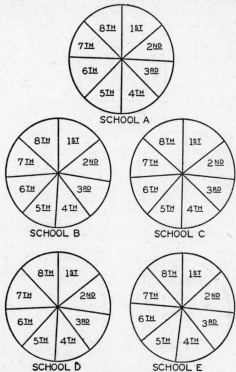

Figure 12. Comparison of class sizes in all schools given in Table IV.

for the two schools. Obviously, this method of graphical representation may not be extended indefinitely to more and more separate schools (or entities of whatever kind) because if many more bars are added the graph merely becomes confusing instead of enlightening.

More Complex Information by Means of the "Pie" Graph

Table IV includes the data for five different schools in the same community. It would be very difficult to read a bar graph which attempted to present all of the informa-

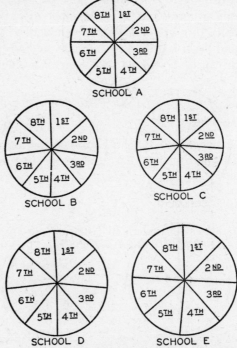

Figure 13. Comparison of class sizes and total
school population in all schools given
in Table IV.

tion of this table by means of bars. The use of the circle graph will overcome much of this difficulty. In this case, however, it is necessary also to decide whether the relative sizes of the total school populations is to be represented, or only the relative division into grades. In Figure 12, circles of the same size are used; each one indicates the proportionate number of pupils in each grade, but no indication is given of the total number of pupils in each school. In Figure 13, circles of different sizes are used, the areas being proportional to the total school population, and the angles being proportional to the number of pupils in each grade. While this graph is more satisfactory than a bar graph would be, it is still clear that the amount of information which can be portrayed by means of a single graph is limited.

Variations of the Bar Graph With More Than Two Quantities

If the two sets of data are of contrasting types, bar graphs with the base line down the center, instead of at the

TABLE V

Enrollments in Public and Catholic Schools, in Each Grade, in a Given Community

Grade	Enrollment		Per Cent of Total for Grade	
	Public	Catholic	Public	Catholic
1	3426	1559	68.7	31.3
2	3120	1651	65.4	34.6
3	3059	1750	63.6	36.4
4	2976	1764	62.8	37.2
5	2995	1800	62.5	37.5
6	2923	1654	63.9	36.1
7	3135	1530	67.2	32.8
8	3011	1406	68.2	31.8
9	3674	511	87.8	12.2
10	2970	441	87.1	12.9
11	2481	407	85.9	14.1
12	2226	367	85.8	14.2

left, are sometimes advisable. For example, the data of Table V show the number of pupils in each grade in the public and the Catholic schools of a given city. Instead of using two parallel bars to represent, for example, the first grade of each type of school, the method shown in Figure 14 may be employed. In this case, the bars to the left of

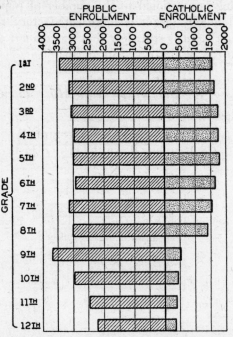

Figure 14. A bar graph with the base line down the center.

the center line represent the public-school population, and those at the right, the Catholic-school enrollments. This method is, perhaps, a little superior to that illustrated by Figure 15, in which continuous bars are drawn for each grade, the left half representing one type of school and the right half the other type, with variation in the crosshatching. If only the relative sizes of the enrollments in each grade in each type of school must be shown, Figure 16 is to be preferred. This figure is based on the percentages given in Table V.

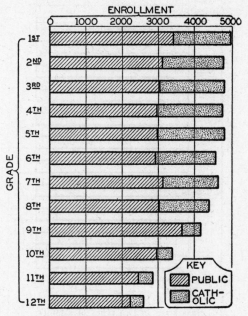

Figure 15. A bar graph with continuous bars.

A variation of the double bar with the dividing line in the center has recently been introduced to represent data of the type given in Table V. This graph consists of the figures indicating the nature of the subject matter of the data. For example, in this case, simplified figures of school children might be employed, each figure representing so many units. This type of graph is illustrated in Figure 17. As pointed out before, the exact size of the quantities cannot be determined with precision from the graph; but this disadvantage is often outweighed by the interest aroused by the pictorial representation.

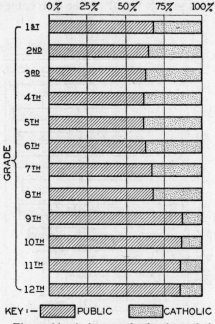

Figure 16. A bar graph showing relative class sizes in two types of schools.

Additional Uses of the Bar Graph

Sometimes the bar graph is employed to show more than just the quantities involved. For example, Table VI presents data on the scores earned by the fifth-grade pupils in five schools in a given community on a standardized test. By examining the table in detail, one can discover the highest score earned by any pupil in a given school, as well as the lowest score. In addition, the medians and quartiles

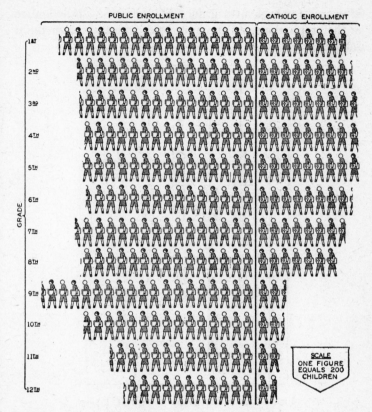

Figure 17. A combination of pictorial representation and the bar
graph with the center base line.

— both first and third — are indicated. In Figure 18 these
same items of information are presented in graphical form.
In this figure, the heavy part of the bar represents the
scores between the first and third quartile for each group.
The light horizontal line cutting the bar indicates the location of the median for each school. The extended single
lines, above and below the bars, show the complete range

of scores for each fifth grade. Thus, from an examination of the graph alone, it is possible to deduce facts such as the following: School C had a higher median score than any of

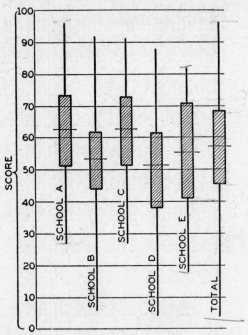

Figure 18. A bar graph comparing highest and lowest scores, medians, first and third quartiles of scores on a test taken by students in five schools.

the others, followed by School A, while the lowest median is found in School D. Likewise, with respect to the largest complete spread of scores, School B ranks first, and School D, second. In addition, it is seen that the variability — or dispersion — is greater in School E than in the others, since there is a wider spread between the first and third quartiles.

The graph includes the same items of information for the total group, in order that each school may be compared with the total, as well as with other individual schools.

TABLE VI

Scores Earned on a Standardized Test by the Fifth-Grade
Pupils in Five Schools in a Particular City

Score	School A	School B	School C	School D	School E	Total
90–99	3	1	1			5
80–89	8	3	7	1	6	25
70–79	15	5	16	2	18	56
60–69	22	12	21	19	14	88
50–59	17	25	20	20	15	97
40–49	12	16	10	14	16	68
30–39	4	8	2	9	8	31
20–29	3	2	1	7	7	20
10–19		1		4	6	11
0– 9		1		1		2
Total	84	74	78	77	90	403
Median	62.73	53.60	62.86	51.75	55.33	57.16
Q_1	51.17	44.06	51.30	38.05	40.94	45.55
Q_3	73.33	62.08	72.81	61.45	70.83	68.32

Chapter VII

SPECIALIZED TYPES OF GRAPHS

In the two previous chapters, we have dealt with the comparison of magnitudes by means of graphical representation, first demonstrating the various ways in which two magnitudes can be compared, and then considering the more desirable methods of comparing more than two magnitudes on the same graph. Two special cases of this type of comparison remain: those in which the magnitudes are distinguished by differences in space, or geography; and those in which they are distinguished by differences in time, or order of occurrence.

Spatial or Map Comparison of Magnitudes

In some instances, it is desirable to show graphically the difference in some measurable trait or some characteristic capable of being counted, or measured in some other numerical quantity, between different geographical areas. For example, the total area involved might be the United States, and the smaller areas between which the comparison is to be made might be single states, or sections including several contiguous states. Or the total area might be a single city, and the smaller areas to be compared might be wards, or school districts, or any other convenient and meaningful unit. Such types of comparisons are usually shown in one of two ways. The first is the method in which the differences are shown by means of variations in the crosshatching of the areas in question. The second is the method in which each unit — or convenient multiple of a unit — is represented by a dot or other significant mark on the map itself. The method to be used in a particular case may depend largely upon the purpose of the statistician who makes the graph.

As an example of the first method of map representation, the data of Table VII are presented. The figures there given are based on data obtained in the National Survey of the Education of Teachers. Of course, an examination of the table reveals all of the pertinent facts concerning the states; and the introduction of sectional groupings of the states also brings out certain sectional differences. However, Figure 19, based on this table, also makes clear in a somewhat more graphic manner many of the same facts. It will be noted that in transferring the information from the table to the graph, some convenient grouping of the variations must be determined. In this case, the groupings are by variations of ten per cent — 0.0 to 9.9; 10.0 to 19.9, etc., up to the final group of 40.0 per cent and over. An examination of the map makes clear that the highest percentages of new teachers, by states, are found in the Mountain section, especially in the northern part; and the next highest in the West Central Section, especially the West North Central.

A second example of this type of map graph, based on a smaller geographic area, is shown in Figure 20. This map represents the mental disease rates of the patients from a particular city in public and private hospitals in the state. The method of grouping is somewhat different from that in Figure 19. In Figure 20 the city is divided into small political areas. The one-sixth of all these areas having the highest mental disease rates are colored black, with white dots, irrespective of the exact rates. Thus, the rates in this group vary from 163.88 to 429.90. The next one-sixth of

TABLE VII

Per Cent of Elementary Teachers Employed in 1930–31 Who Were New to Their Positions, by States

New England —	*11.9*	West North Central —	*34.5*
Maine	21.1	Minnesota	31.1
New Hampshire	18.6	Iowa	32.9
Vermont	24.5	Missouri	20.7
Massachusetts	7.5	North Dakota	46.5
Rhode Island	6.4	South Dakota	45.2
Connecticut	10.2	Nebraska	39.0
		Kansas	35.7
Middle Atlantic —	*12.8*	West South Central —	*24.3*
New York	13.3	Arkansas	27.3
New Jersey	8.6	Louisiana	14.4
Pennsylvania	13.7	Oklahoma	32.6
		Texas	24.8
South Atlantic —	*16.9*	Mountain —	*35.8*
Delaware	16.9	Montana	41.9
Maryland	9.3	Idaho	40.0
District of Columbia	6.3	Wyoming	41.1
Virginia	17.2	Colorado	38.2
West Virginia	8.7	New Mexico	29.9
North Carolina	20.8	Arizona	28.8
South Carolina	18.3	Utah	21.5
Georgia	17.0	Nevada	40.0
Florida	18.6		
East North Central —	*20.0*	Pacific —	*20.0*
Ohio	14.7	Washington	26.1
Indiana	13.9	Oregon	27.1
Illinois	24.1	California	15.4
Michigan	22.7		
Wisconsin	28.4		
East South Central —	*17.8*	*United States —*	*20.5*
Kentucky	15.7		
Tennessee	16.3		
Alabama	18.7		
Mississippi	27.2		

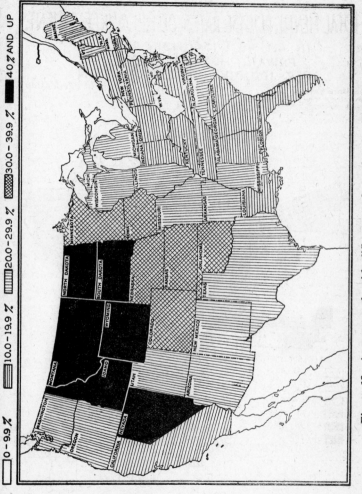

0-9.9% ▦ 10.0-19.9% ▥ 20.0-29.9% ▨ 30.0-39.9% ▦ 40% AND UP

Figure 19. A map graph with differences shown by crosshatching.

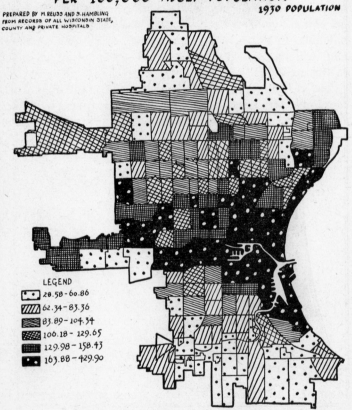

MAP I

TOTAL MENTAL DISEASE RATES OF MILWAUKEE PATIENTS
IN ALL 48 WISCONSIN PUBLIC AND
PRIVATE HOSPITALS 1925-1938
PER 100,000 ADULT POPULATION

1930 POPULATION

PREPARED BY M. REUSS AND S. HAMBLING
FROM RECORDS OF ALL WISCONSIN STATE,
COUNTY AND PRIVATE HOSPITALS

LEGEND
28.58 – 60.86
62.34 – 83.36
83.89 – 104.34
106.18 – 129.65
129.98 – 158.43
163.88 – 429.90

Figure 20. Another type of map graph.

the small areas, in terms of mental disease rates, are given the next darkest crosshatching. For this group the rates vary from 129.98 to 158.45. The remaining sixths of the total group are also each differentiated from the others. In the group with the smallest mental disease rates, from 28.58 to 60.86, the areas are white, with black dots. There are an equal number of small areas for each type of cross-hatching. In so far as the areas are approximately equal, the map will be divided into about six equal parts, according to the mental disease rates.

The second type of map graph, with individual cases represented by dots or other marks, is illustrated by Figure 21. This is a map of a county of Wisconsin, divided into

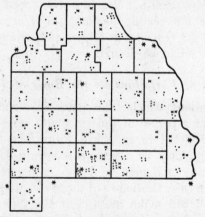

Figure 21. A map graph with individual cases represented by dots and other marks.

towns. Each star (*) designates a high school attended by the graduates of the rural schools in a particular year. It is to be noted that eight such stars are within the county, and four others are just outside the boundaries, in contiguous counties. Each dot on the map represents an eighth-grade graduate of the rural schools who attended high school the following fall. Each x represents an eighth-grade graduate who did not enroll in any high school. From such a map certain deductions may be drawn concerning the effect of distance upon high-school attendance of rural-school graduates. Thus, in certain towns, where high schools are convenient, all such graduates were enrolled in high school. In others, where the graduates could not reach a high school except by traveling a considerable distance, a much smaller percentage was enrolled. On the other hand, it is also clear that in certain towns, even with a high school conveniently located, a fairly large proportion of the eighth-grade graduates did not see fit to attend. Such a spot map is valuable if one wishes to point out clearly districts where high-school facilities are not readily available, and also where such facilities are not reaching as large a proportion of the rural graduates as might be desired.

Comparison of Variations on the Basis of Time

The variations which take place in some measurable quantity over a period of time in many cases can be very effectively depicted in graphical form. The time interval used as a unit may be a year, a month, a day, or even a smaller period; or it may be a five- or ten-year period, or more. In each case, the maker of the graph attempts to select a unit which will make most clear the type of variation which he has found in the data. An example of this type of graph is shown in Figure 22, based on the data of Table VIII. This table gives for each year from 1890 to 1939 the index of purchasing power of teachers' salaries in the United States. The index for each year was obtained from the index of the cost of living, as furnished by the Bureau of Labor Statistics, and the average salaries of teachers, as given by the Biennial Survey of Education.

TABLE VIII

Index of Purchasing Power of Teachers' Salaries, 1890–1939*

Year	Index 1913 = 1.00	Year	Index 1913 = 1.00
1890	.65	1915	1.01
1891	.69	1916	.95
1892	.70	1917	.83
1893	.73	1918	.71
1894	.78	1919	.77
1895	.79	1920	.82
1896	.78	1921	1.21
1897	.80	1922	1.36
1898	.82	1923	1.37
1899	.82	1924	1.40
1900	.82	1925	1.39
1901	.84	1926	1.42
1902	.84	1927	1.47
1903	.83	1928	1.57
1904	.87	1929	1.60
1905	.90	1930	1.69
1906	.91	1931	1.91
1907	.90	1932	2.07
1908	.98	1933	1.96
1909	1.03	1934	1.75
1910	1.01	1935	1.73
1911	1.00	1936	1.75
1912	1.01	1937	1.75
1913	1.00	1938	1.83
1914	1.00	1939	1.89

* Data for 1890 to 1926 from Research Bulletin of the National Education Association, May, 1927. Additional years based on Index of Cost of Living of Bureau of Labor Statistics, and average annual salaries of teachers, from issues of Biennial Survey of Education.

For earlier years, the table is that presented in a Research Bulletin of the National Education Association; for later years the data were taken from the same basic sources. The graph shows in much more impressive fashion than the table,

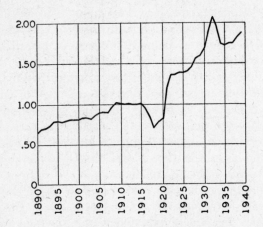

Figure 22. Variations in quantities over a period of time depicted graphically.

the drop in purchasing power of teachers' salaries during the First World War, and the two periods of rapid increase up to 1932, several years after the beginning of the depression period; following 1932 there is a decrease in purchasing power, with another slight upswing beginning in 1938.

While the few examples given do not begin to exhaust the possibilities of graphical representation of data, they have furnished illustrations of most of the typical kinds of graphs based on comparison of magnitudes or quantities. The principal points to be kept in mind by those who read graphs is that in each case the statistician is attempting to present his data in a form which will make their meaning more clear; and that any type of data which can be expressed in numerical form may also be represented by some appropriate kind of graph.

Graphical Representation of Distributions

There remains one very important kind of graphical representation which is frequently seen in educational and social-science reports; namely, the graphical representation of a distribution of data of a continuous type. Table IX presents such a distribution of test scores earned by a group of pupils. It is to be noted that, as explained in an earlier chapter, the scores are grouped into intervals — in this case, intervals of ten units. Thus, all pupils who earned scores from 40 to 49 are counted and the number is indicated at that interval in the table; and similarly for those who earned scores from 30 to 39, from 60 to 69, etc. In one sense, this table could be represented in a graph made up of separate bars, either horizontal or vertical. But, in another sense, this type of data differs from the kind ordinarily so represented in that the data are continuous. In other words, at least theoretically, a pupil could have a score of 39.9 or even of 39.999; that is, any particular integral or decimal score is theoretically possible. For that reason, the graph is usually made continuous, without a definite break between the various segments or groups.

One method of representing the data of Table IX in a graph is shown in Figure 23. In this case, the bars are all made of the same width, and their heights are proportional to the number of cases found at each interval; but no space is left between them. This type of graph has the advantage that each case or individual involved is represented by a particular area, and the total area under the graph is equal to the total number of cases or individuals. Where data simply represent a particular sample of pupils, as in this set of data, or a particular sample of some other units, and no attempt is made to deduce anything for a larger group, this kind of graph is to be preferred.

In many cases, however, the particular group of individuals involved in the sample measured are important only because of the deductions concerning a larger total population which may be drawn. Thus, the pupils included in Table IX might be thought of as having been drawn from

TABLE IX

Distribution of Scores Earned by 360 Pupils on a Test; and Cumulative Frequency Distribution

Score Interval	Frequency	Cumulative Frequency
160–169.9	3	360
150–159.9	6	357
140–149.9	10	351
130–139.9	18	341
120–129.9	25	323
110–119.9	36	298
100–109.9	43	262
90– 99.9	65	219
80– 89.9	50	154
70– 79.9	48	104
60– 69.9	22	56
50– 59.9	20	34
40– 49.9	11	14
30– 39.9	2	3
20– 29.9	1	1
Total	360	

a much larger total population of pupils of the same grade level throughout the country. In such a case, it becomes desirable to try to discover what would be the distribution of all of these pupils on the same test. As a first step in that direction, a graph such as that shown in Figure 24

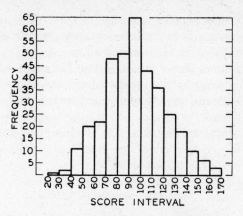

Figure 23. A graphical representation of a distribution of data.

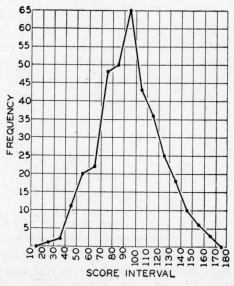

Figure 24. Curve showing a sample distribution.

may be constructed. In this case, a mark is placed at the middle of the space represented by the interval, and at the height indicated by the number of pupils in the interval. These points are then connected, and the graph is extended to the zero point at the middle of the interval next below the first one and next above the last one in which any cases are found.

A final step may be taken if it is assumed that the slight irregularities in this curve are due only to the particular sample included in the table. In such a case, these irregularities are eliminated, and the curve is drawn as in Figure 25.

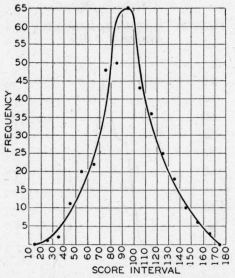

Figure 25. The curve in Figure 24 smoothed out.

This figure does not really represent the data of Table IX; however, it does represent what the statistician deduces would be the shape of the distribution if larger and larger numbers of pupils were tested, until finally the entire group of pupils of that grade were included. In this instance, the smoothing of the curve has been done very simply and directly, in order to illustrate the graphic result only. In actual practice, of course, the statistician would require more data, and would smooth the curve in accordance with definite statistical procedures, until he was reasonably sure that he could justify the final graph as the one most probably representing the distribution of the entire population on the particular measure.

The Cumulative Frequency Graph

A variation of the last mentioned type of graph is one in which the height of the curve at any point is determined,

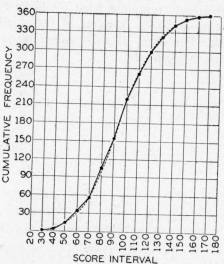

Figure 26. A cumulative frequency graph.

not by the frequency or number of cases in the particular interval, but by the accumulation of all frequencies up to that point. In the last column of Table IX the cumulative frequencies for each interval are shown. These are obtained by adding together all frequencies in lower intervals, and the interval in question. The frequency for the next interval is then added to this total, to obtain the accumulation at that point; and so on for each additional interval. When these cumulative frequencies are represented on a graph, Figure 26 is the result. The major advantage of such a graph is that one can read from it directly the number of pupils who made a certain score, or less. When the cumulative frequencies are taken directly from the table, usually an irregular curve results, as shown by the solid line in Figure 26. Here again, the statistician may feel that he is justified in smoothing the curve — with proper statistical procedures — in order better to represent what would be expected to occur if a more complete sampling of the population had been obtained. The effect of such smoothing is shown in the dotted line in Figure 26.

Chapter VIII

COMPARABLE SCORES

A very useful concept in modern statistical practice is that of comparable scores. It is made necessary by the fact that many tests, rating scales, and other measuring instruments used by educators and social workers today result in scores or ratings which are not in themselves entirely meaningful. For example, a particular test or scale may be so constructed that the scores which will be earned by a normal group of individuals for whom it is suitable will run from, say, 5 to 30. Another test, in a different field, or even in the same field, may be so constructed that the scores earned by the same group of individuals will run from 90 to 220. Obviously, a score of 25 on the first test — since it is close to the maximum expected — will stand for a higher ranking than a score of 125 on the second test — which is near the minimum expected. The differences in the size of scores will be due to the simplicity or complexity of the test, to the number of questions included, to the time allowed in taking the test, to the amount of credit given for each question, and to many other factors. None of these factors, in themselves, are vital to the trait or characteristic which is being measured. It is clear, then, that if the results of such measurements are to be interpreted correctly, some information in addition to the actual or "raw" scores — the scores earned by the individuals on the scale employed in the test — must be given.

Conceivably, one might in every case examine the complete distribution of scores earned by a particular group of pupils, or by the total number of individuals to whom the test or scale has been applied, as in the case of a standardized test. By such an examination, he might arrive at a correct interpretation of the value or significance of the score of an individual, or of the scores of a number of individuals. However, as we have already pointed out, the statistician likes to express the results in a form which is more easily interpreted, and which has some sort of standard or commonly accepted meaning. There are a number of these commonly accepted methods of expressing the meaning of a particular score in such a way that it is unnecessary to know all of the facts about the distribution of scores of the group in order to make a correct interpretation. The common name of such a method of expressing the mean of a score is *comparable score*. Among the various kinds of comparable scores commonly used are *percentile scores, standard scores or z-scores, T-scores*.

The Percentile Method

The use and interpretation of *percentile scores* can probably be made clear most easily by an example. In Table X are given the scores of a group of college freshmen on a test. In the third column are shown the cumulative frequencies — that is, the sum of all cases up to and including the particular class or score interval involved. For example, in the first class interval, 110.0–119.9, only 1 case is found; in the next interval, 120.0–129.9, there are 2; therefore, up to and including the second interval, there are a total of 3. Similarly, up to and including the interval 160.0–169.9 there were 99 cases; in the next interval, 170.0–179.9, there were 46 more; therefore, up to and including the latter interval, there were a total of 145. The same procedure is used throughout the table. The last column of this table gives what are called the cumulative-percentage frequencies. Thus,

TABLE X

Distribution of Scores Earned by 500 Students on a Test;
Cumulative Frequency Distribution; and Cumulative
Percentage Distribution

Class Interval (Scores)	No. of Students (Frequency)	Cumulative Frequency	Cumulative Percentage
270.0–279.9	2	500	100.0
260.0–269.9	4	498	99.6
250.0–259.9	10	494	98.8
240.0–249.9	18	484	96.8
230.0–239.9	30	466	93.2
220.0–229.9	42	436	87.2
210.0–219.9	50	394	78.8
200.0–209.9	61	344	68.8
190.0–199.9	76	283	56.6
180.0–189.9	62	207	41.4
170.0–179.9	46	145	29.0
160.0–169.9	40	99	19.8
150.0–159.9	32	59	11.8
140.0–149.9	17	27	5.4
130.0–139.9	7	10	2.0
120.0–129.9	2	3	0.6
110.0–119.9	1	1	0.2

Total 500   (Mean, 196.0; Sigma, 29.0)

up to and including the interval last mentioned, there were
145 cases; since the total number involved is 500, and
since 145 is equal to 29.0 per cent of that total number, or
500, it is said that the cumulative percentage frequency up
to the top of that class interval is 29.0. Similarly, since there
were 466 cases up to and including the interval 230.0–239.9,
and since 466 is equal to 93.2 per cent of the total number,
the cumulative percentage frequency to that point is 93.2.
The remainder of the column is obtained in the same way —
by dividing the cumulative frequency at each interval by the
total number of cases.

A cumulative percentage frequency graph is now constructed, based on the data of Table X, and shown in the left half of Figure 27. It is to be observed that this is the same as the cumulative frequency graph explained in the previous chapter, except that the heights of the curve at the various points is referred to a percentage scale on the vertical axis. The cumulative frequency scale is also shown on the same axis for comparison. It now becomes clear that the percentage value of any score, or the score value of any percentage, may be read, at least roughly, from the graph. Thus it is seen, for example, that the 20th percentage point corresponds roughly to the point 170 on the horizontal axis. This percentage value corresponding to a particular score is spoken of as a *percentile rank*. Therefore we would say that the score 170 has a percentile rank of 20. Or, inversely, we say that the "20th percentile" for this distribution is the score 170. This means that 20 per cent of the individuals included in the distribution had scores below 170. In the same way, since the score 225 corresponds roughly to the percentile value 83.0, we would say that 225 has a percentile rank of 83, and that the 83rd percentile is 225.

Of course, there is a mathematical procedure by means of which the exact score corresponding to any given percentile, and the exact percentile corresponding to any given score, may be computed. This procedure need not be explained here, since the purpose is to show the meaning of the concept, and not the statistical techniques used in computation. It is true, however, that in many instances where it is desired to translate all scores of an entire group to approximate percentiles, a graph similar to Figure 27 is constructed — probably much larger, and on much finer graph paper — and the percentiles are read off as accurately as possible.

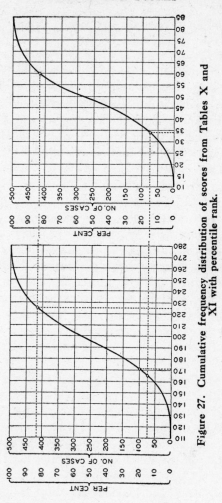

Figure 27. Cumulative frequency distribution of scores from Tables X and XI with percentile rank.

Comparing Scores on Two Tests by the Percentile Method

Part of the value of the percentile method consists in the fact that it may be used with any distribution, and in each case a given percentile score has the same significance. Thus, the 43rd percentile would mean that score, or point on the scale, below which 43 per cent of all individuals involved happened to fall, no matter what the actual scores might be.

TABLE XI

Distribution of Scores Earned by 500 Students on a Second Test; Cumulative Frequency Distribution; and Cumulative Percentage Distribution

Class Interval (Scores)	No. of Students (Frequency)	Cumulative Frequency	Cumulative Percentage
80.0–84.9	3	500	100.0
75.0–79.9	6	497	99.4
70.0–74.9	12	491	98.2
65.0–69.9	25	479	93.8
60.0–64.9	38	454	90.8
55.0–59.9	51	416	83.2
50.0–54.9	71	365	73.0
45.0–49.5	90	294	53.8
40.0–44.9	69	204	40.8
35.0–39.9	50	135	27.0
30.0–34.9	40	85	17.0
25.0–29.9	24	45	9.0
20.0–24.9	11	21	4.2
15.0–19.9	6	10	2.0
10.0–14.9	4	4	0.8

Total 500   (Mean, 47.5; Sigma, 13.0)

A further advantage is that scores earned on dissimilar tests may be compared directly when transformed to percentiles. Table XI gives another set of scores, earned by the same

500 individuals, on an entirely different test. In this case, the lowest score is 10, and the highest is 89. If the same individual earned a score of 165 on the first test considered, and a score of 34 on the second test, it is not immediately clear whether he did better on the first, or on the second, or about the same on both tests. But when Figure 27 is consulted, it is discovered that his score of 165 is equivalent to a percentile rank of 15.8. By comparison with the right half of Figure 27, Based on Table XI, it is found that a score of 34 is roughly equivalent to a percentile rank of 15.4. Thus it is seen that this individual stood in about the same position on both tests.

Other similar comparisons may be made between the two graphs. Thus, the score of 225 on the first test was found above to be equal roughly, to a percentile rank of 83.0. By examining the second graph, it is found that the 83rd percentile is equivalent to a score of about 60. In other words, one who earned a score of 225 on the first test did as well as one who earned a score of 60 on the second test. In the same way, for each score earned on either test there may be found a corresponding score on the other test which represents approximately — exactly, if done by formula — the same position in the group. Thus the advantage of the percentile method is that it permits the translation of scores attained on various tests, scales, or other measuring instruments to values which will always have the same significance, irrespective of the range or nature of the original scores.

The Standard-Score Method

While the percentile method is valuable, it is, after all, only a counting method, just as the median is a counting measure of central tendency. For certain purposes a more strictly mathematical method of obtaining comparable scores is more desirable. In such cases the *standard score* or *z-score* is frequently used — or other types of scores derived from the standard score. To illustrate the meaning of this type of score, the data of Tables X and XI are used. The frequency distributions, shown in the second column of the two tables, are also represented in the two graphs of Figure 28. These graphs are of the type explained in the previous chapter, with the scores arranged on the horizontal axis, and the number of cases in each interval shown on the vertical axis.

Attention is first called to the upper graph in Figure 28, based on the data of Table X. In the table it is indicated

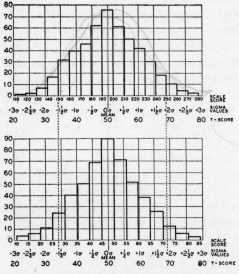

Figure 28. Standard scores and T-scores.

that the mean of the distribution is 196.0. A line is therefore drawn through the graph, bisecting the horizontal axis at the score value 196.0. The table also gives the standard deviation, or sigma, of the distribution as 29.0. Both mean and sigma, of course, have been computed by the use of the proper statistical procedures, as discussed in an earlier chapter. As stated in that discussion, the value of sigma, or 29.0 in this case, is expressed in terms of the score or scalar values of this particular distribution. It therefore can be indicated on the graph. Thus, the expression "plus 1 sigma" means a distance on the scale above the mean, and above the mean by the amount of 1 sigma. Since the value of sigma in this case is 29.0, and the value of the mean is 196.0, the point "plus 1 sigma" must coincide with the point on the graph of 196.0 plus 29.0, or 225.0. In the figure it has been so indicated.

By similar reasoning, other points corresponding to other values of sigma, both above and below the mean, may be indicated. Thus, the point "minus 2 sigmas" will correspond to the point 196.0 (the mean) minus twice the value of sigma (2 times 29.0), or 196.0 minus 58.0, which is 138.0. The points on the scale which correspond to successive half values of sigma, above and below the mean, are as follows:

Values of Sigma	Plus	Minus
0 (the mean)	196.0	
½ sigma	210.5	181.5
1 sigma	225.0	167.0
1½ sigma	239.5	152.5
2 sigmas	254.0	138.0
2½ sigmas	268.5	123.5
3 sigmas	283.0	109.0

All of these six points above the mean, and six points below the mean, have been indicated on the graph of these data, and are noted on a scale on the horizontal axis placed below the score scale.

By examination of the graph, it should be clear that the scale is independent of the actual score values, but corresponds to them. This scale also has the advantage that it is dependent on the exact score made by every individual in the distribution, since both the mean and the sigma take into account, in their computation, the exact score of each case involved; and since the standard score is derived from the values of the mean and sigma. From an examination of the two scales — the scale for the scores on the test, and the scale for sigma values above and below the mean — it is also clear that there is a one-to-one correspondence between the two. That is, for every score on the score scale, there is some value of sigma — either plus or minus; either integral or decimal — which corresponds to it. In the same way, for every value of sigma, there is a score corresponding. Thus, for example, the score 250 corresponds to the sigma value 1.86; similarly, the score 150 corresponds to the sigma value —1.59. In actual practice, the sigma values are found, not by reference to a graph, but by means of a formula; but this procedure need not be explained here. The graph is chiefly valuable in demonstrating the correspondence between these two types of scores. This kind of score, measured by the distance, in sigmas, above or below the mean, is called a *standard score,* or, sometimes, a *z-score.*

Attention is now called to the lower graph of Figure 28, based on the scores of Table XI. In this case, as in the first graph, the mean (47.5) is indicated; also, the position of the sigma values, by ½ sigmas, above and below the mean (sigma was found, as indicated in the table, to be equal to 13.0). In order to bring out more clearly the interpretation of these standard scores, this second graph has been made to correspond to the first in the location of the mean, and of the positions of the sigma values above and below the mean. Thus, for example, it is seen that the position of plus 1 sigma (mean, 47.5, plus 1 sigma, 13.0) is 60.5; and that this point falls directly below the value 225.0, or plus

1 sigma, on the upper graph. In other words, a score of 225.0 would be expressed by a standard score of 1.00 for the first distribution; and a score of 60.5 would be expressed by a standard score of 1.00 for the second. Similarly, a score of 123.5, on the first distribution, has a standard score of –2.50; on the second distribution, the score 15.0 has a standard score of –2.50. This standard score of –2.50 (or any other standard score) has a very definite significance with respect to the relative position of a student earning it; and this significance remains, irrespective of the amount of the score actually earned on the test.

Translating Scores From One Scale to Another

This last mode of comparison leads to another type of comparable score which is sometimes used. If it happens that the statistician would prefer to have his scores in some form other than standard scores, he can readily transform them. Such preference may spring from the fact that the standard scores may be either positive or negative, leading to some difficulty in use and interpretation. It may also be that he is accustomed to the interpretation of the scores earned on one test — say, that of Table XI — but is not so familiar with the scores of the other test — that of Table X. In such a case he may wish to translate the scores earned by all students on the test of Table X into their equivalent scores on the test of Table XI. The graphs in Figure 28 show readily how this may be done. It is only necessary to translate the scores first into standard scores, and then to find the scores in the second test which correspond to those standard scores. Of course, in practice, the procedure is facilitated by the use of a formula, which is beyond the scope of the present discussion. The graph shows what the results would be. Thus, the score of 250 in the upper graph was found to be equivalent to a standard score of 1.86. Carrying this line down into the lower graph, it is found that a standard score of 1.86 is equivalent to a score of 71.7. In other words, a score of 250 on the test reported in Table X is equivalent to a score of 71.7 on the test reported in Table XI. Similarly, the score 150 on the upper graph had a standard score value of −1.59; carried down to the lower graph, this is found to correspond to a score of 26.8. Thus, a score of 150 on the first test is equivalent to a score of 26.8 on the second test.

The T-Score

A slight modification of the procedures so far described is sometimes used to translate scores to *T-scores*. (In a more limited sense, the T-score in its original use referred back to the mean for pupils at a certain level in school on standardized tests; but the more extended meaning here given to it is also found in educational writings and will illustrate its significance.) Below the standard-score scale of each graph in Figure 28 will be noted another scale, for T-scores. This scale has the special features that the mean is always 50, and the value of sigma is 10. In other words, when a T-score equivalent is given, one can see immediately whether it corresponds to a positive or negative standard score (that is, whether it is above or below the mean of the original distribution) by simply noting if it is above or below 50. In addition, one can determine also at once how far above or below the mean it will be, in terms of sigmas; thus, 40 is 1 sigma below the mean (50 minus 10), 70 is 2 sigmas above the mean (50 plus [2 times 10]), etc. This type of transformation is useful when the statistician desires to avoid the negative numbers of the standard scores, and when he is not sufficiently familiar with the significance of the scores of any particular test used to justify translating scores from other distributions to the scale of that test.

Chapter IX

CORRELATION

Correlation is one of the most valuable tools of the statistician. A large amount of statistical interpretation may be carried out, to be sure, by the analysis of data obtained by a single measure for each case or individual involved. But sooner or later one is going to be confronted with a problem in which he has obtained two or more measures for each of the constituent entities with which he is dealing. Thus, if a pupil has been given one test, it is likely that a score on a second test will be available — and even a third, fourth, and fifth. If he has a grade in one subject, he will also have a grade in a second subject, and a third, and a fourth. Or the social worker who is studying the vital statistics of a state will find that he has obtained the birth rate for each county in the state, and also the death rate for each county. Or when he has obtained a measure of the incidence of crime, or of insanity, or of feeble-mindedness for the various wards or other divisions of a city, he will also find that he has available a measure of the density of population, or the average rental, or some other significant index of economic status, for the same divisions.

In any of these cases, and many others, it is just as interesting and important to discover if there is any relationship between the various measures for the same individual (pupil, county, ward, etc.) as it is to tabulate and analyze the data for the group on some single characteristic. In fact, in many cases, the determination of the relationship between traits, or scores, or rates, or other measures, is much more important than any possible analysis of the distributions of single measures. In order that a study of such possible relationships be made, it is necessary to understand something about the nature of the concept of correlation. At this point again, the statistician is not satisfied simply to indicate such relationship in a general way; he insists on a procedure which will give in a single compact number the nature and amount of their relationship.

TABLE XII

Comparison of Scores Earned by Ten Pupils on Various Tests

Pupil	Test 1	Test 2	Pupil	Test 1	Test 3
B	90	84	A	95	80
D	80	76	B	90	77
E	75	70	C	85	74
A	95	82	D	80	71
G	65	87	E	75	68
J	50	74	F	70	65
F	70	68	G	65	62
C	85	91	H	60	59
I	55	66	I	55	56
H	60	61	J	50	53

Pupil	Test 1	Test 4	Pupil	Test 1	Test 5
A	95	98	A	95	51
B	90	91	B	90	55
C	85	84	C	85	59
D	80	77	D	80	63
E	75	70	E	75	67
F	70	63	F	70	71
G	65	56	G	65	75
H	60	49	H	60	79
I	55	42	I	55	83
J	50	35	J	50	87

TABLE XII (Continued)

Comparison of Scores Earned by Ten Pupils on Various Tests

Pupil	Test 1	Test 6	Pupil	Test 1	Test 7
A	95	72	A	95	90
B	90	90	B	90	62
C	85	65	C	85	84
D	80	82	D	80	71
E	75	87	E	75	60
F	70	87	F	70	87
G	65	82	G	65	51
H	60	65	H	60	68
I	55	90	I	55	85
J	50	72	J	50	79

Pupil	Test 1	Test 8	Pupil	Test 1	Test 9
A	95	97	A	95	82
B	90	94	B	90	76
C	85	86	C	85	98
D	80	85	D	80	72
E	75	84	E	75	56
F	70	76	F	70	61
G	65	75	G	65	93
H	60	70	H	60	54
I	55	61	I	55	52
J	50	60	J	50	80

Relationship as Revealed by Examination of Tables

In order to make the problem somewhat more concrete, the data of Table XII are introduced. To simplify the comparisons, each distribution is limited to ten cases. The table gives a series of scores earned by these ten pupils on nine different examinations. In each pair of columns, the first represents the scores made by these individuals on the same test — called Test 1. The second column of each pair represents the scores made by the same pupils on some other test — Test 2, Test 3, etc. Even a casual examination of these pairs of columns makes it clear that there is considerable variation in the relationship between the pairs of scores involved. Thus, in some cases, as in the comparison of Tests 1 and 3, those who made high scores on one test of the pair also made high scores on the other, and as the scores of individuals on the first test are found to be lower, so also are their scores on the second test. In other cases, as in the comparison of Tests 1 and 5, those with high scores on one test have low scores on the second; and those with low scores on the first have higher scores on the second. In some cases, also as in the comparison of Tests 1 and 6, there appears to be no regularity in the variation. Thus a pupil with a high score, such as 90, on Test 6 may have either a high or a low score on Test 1; and a pupil with a low score, such as 72, on Test 6, may also have either a high or a low score on Test 1.

This type of casual comparison may readily be made in these cases, in which only ten individuals are involved; even in such a case, when the scores of one test are not arranged in order, as in the first pair of columns, the comparison is not readily made. Whenever more cases are involved such comparison by inspection becomes increasingly difficult. At any event, such inspection does not yield a result in the form of a single measure of relationship, and therefore does not satisfy the statistician, who desires to state everything, so far as possible, in compact form.

Graphical Illustration of Correlation

A grasp of the concept of correlation may most simply be obtained by considering certain graphic representations of the data shown in Table XII. In certain of the graphs previously described, it will be remembered that two dimensions were distinguished; one type of information would be represented on the vertical axis, and another on the horizontal axis. In those cases, one axis usually represented the score, the number of cases, or some other measurement of magnitude; and the second axis might stand for certain classes, categories, divisions, etc., of the data, or for a time series. The two axes can equally well be used to represent two different scores or measurements pertaining to particular individuals. This is the form of representation involved in the concept of correlation.

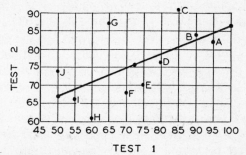

TEST 1

Figure 29. Correlation here is not particularly high.

For the first illustration of this method, the scores on Test 1 and Test 2 for the ten pupils will be taken. In Figure 29 these pairs of scores are represented graphically. For example, for the first pupil in the table, Pupil B, it is found that his score on Test 1 is 90, and his score on Test 2 is 84. Therefore, if one moves along the horizontal axis — representing the Test 1 scores — to the point 90, and then along the vertical axis — representing the Test 2 scores — to the point 84, he will arrive at the point on the graph marked "B." This point locates the standing of this pupil on both tests. Similarly, the second pupil in the table had a score of 80 on Test 1 and 76 on Test 2. The point on the graph which is above 80 on the horizontal axis, and to the right of 76 on the vertical axis represents this pupil's standing, and is marked "D." In the same way, the standing of each pupil on the two tests has been indicated on the graph.

The line drawn in the graph, running from lower left to upper right, represents the best fit obtainable with the points located, in case it were desired to predict a score on the second test from any given score on the first test. This is known as the *line of regression,* or a regression line; more will be said about it in a later chapter. At this point, attention is merely called to the fact that, for this group of data, this line is not an especially good fit to the points located. Since it is not a very good fit, the relationship between the scores on the two tests, or the *correlation,* is not particularly high. Of course, such a general conclusion could also be reached by simply examining the positions of the points on the graph. The entire problem of determining the correlation revolves about the question of how close a fit may actually be obtained between the points located on the graph and such a line of regression drawn through them.

Perfect Positive Correlation

Attention is now called to the second set of comparisons in Table XII, namely those between Test 1 and Test 3. The points determined by these pairs of scores have been represented graphically in Figure 30. In this case, it is seen that the points so located all fall exactly on a straight line. This line is the line of regression, and in this case it fits the data precisely. This means, of course, that any change in the score on Test 1 will be accompanied by a particular change in the score on Test 3. Examination of the table reveals that for every 5 points of increase on Test 1, there will be 3 points of increase on Test 3. Thus, for example, Pupil J has a score of 50 on Test 1 and a score of 53 on Test 3. Pupil I has a score of 55 on Test 1 — just 5 points more than Pupil J. Therefore, on Test 3 we would expect a score 3 points higher than 53, or 56, and we find that such is his score. Going further up the table, we find that

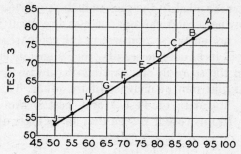

TEST 1

Figure 30. Perfect positive correlation.

Pupil E has a score of 75 on Test 1; this score is 25 points higher than Pupil J, or 5 times 5 points. We would therefore expect that on Test 3 his score would be 5 times 3 points, or 15 points, higher than the score of Pupil J. The latter's score, 53, plus this difference of 15, would be 68; and we find that to be the score of Pupil E, on Test 3.

The particular situation found in Figure 30 seldom occurs in actual data. It is presented here because it is a limiting case. Whenever this type of graph is found, in which all the points representing the individuals involved fall exactly on a straight line, from the smallest score on both to the largest score on both, it is said that there is *perfect positive correlation*. In statistical notation, this would be expressed as,

$$r = 1.00 \text{ (or, possibly, } + 1.00).$$

In other words, the symbol used for the coefficient of correlation is r; and when there is a perfect relationship in the positive direction — so that an increase in one is always accompanied by a consistent increase in the other — the coefficient of correlation is said to be equal to 1.00.

Attention is called to the fact that the precise amount of increase in the second variable, or measure (that is, in this case, the score on the second test in the comparison) is not important — it is only necessary that some given unit of increase in the score in one variable be always found with some particular unit of increase of the other. To represent this point, the data of Test 1 and Test 4 are shown in Figure 31. In this case it is seen that an increase of 5 points

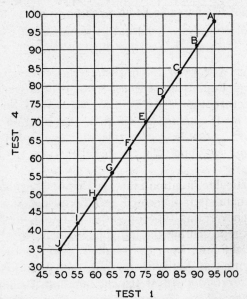

TEST 1

Figure 31. Perfect positive correlation — for every increase of 5 points on Test 1, there is an increase of 7 points in Test 4.

in the score of Test 1 is always accompanied by an increase of 7 points in the score of Test 4. The graph indicates that in this case also the points representing the particular individuals all fall exactly on a straight line. Therefore the correlation is again perfect and positive, and in this case, as in the previous one, is expressed by the statement,

$$r = 1.00.$$

Perfect Negative Correlation

The opposite limiting case of correlation would, of course, be that in which a higher score on one test is associated with a lower score on the second test. This condition is found to be present in the comparison of the scores on Test 1 and Test 5, as shown in Figure 32. In this case,

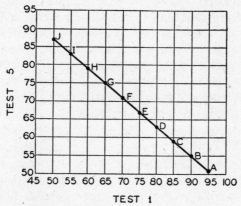

TEST 1

Figure 32. Perfect negative correlation.

it is seen that Pupil A has a score of 95 on Test 1, and of 51 on Test 5. Pupil B has a score just 5 points lower on Test 1, and just 4 points higher on Test 5. Pupil C has a score 5 points lower than Pupil B on Test 1, and 4 points higher on Test 5. In other words, every decrease of 5 points on Test 1 is accompanied by an increase of 4 points on Test 5. In this case there is also perfect correlation, since all points fall on a straight line. However, since an increase in one measure is found with a decrease in the second, the correlation is said to be negative. This is the other limiting case, and is expressed as,

$$r = -1.00.$$

Since there obviously can be nothing beyond perfect agreement, or perfect disagreement, between two sets of measures for the same individuals, all other types of relationship must be expressed by a correlation coefficient which is between −1.00 and 1.00. These two extremes are almost never encountered in actual data obtained from any kind of measurement in statistics dealing with animate beings, so that it is seldom if ever possible to make the kind of accurate prediction which would be possible if the observed data fell exactly on the regression line. Instead, there will merely be a more or less close approximation to a perfect fitting line. In one sense, the coefficient of correlation is a measure of the accuracy of this fit.

Zero Correlation

There is one other situation which may be looked upon, in a sense, as a limiting case, and that is the complete lack of any agreement, either positive or negative, between the two measures. This situation also is seldom found in actual measurement data. An example is shown in the comparison between Test 1 and Test 6, which is represented in Figure 33. In this case it is seen that the pupil with the highest score on Test 1 — Pupil A, with 95 — has a score of 72 on Test 6. Likewise, the pupil with the lowest score on Test 1 — Pupil J, with a score of 50 — also has a score of 72 on Test 6. Similarly, the pupil with the next highest score on Test 1 — Pupil B, with 90 — has a score of 90 on Test 6, which is exactly the same as that of the pupil with the second lowest score on Test 1. Throughout the table and the graph the same situation is found. A pupil standing at any rank from the top on Test 1 has exactly the same score on Test 6 as the pupil who stands at the same rank from

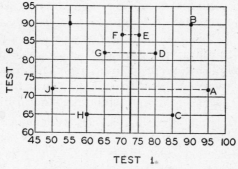

Figure 33. Zero correlation.

the bottom on Test 1. In other words, if one has a score of 65 on Test 6, he may have either a high or a low score on Test 1; if he has a score of 90 on Test 6, he may like-wise have either a high or a low score on Test 1. This is an example of no correlation whatever, and is expressed by the symbols,

$$r = .00.$$

Other Values of the Correlation Coefficient

Neither perfect correlation nor zero correlation is likely to be found among actual data. The nearest approaches to such situations will usually be of the type shown in the comparisons of Test 1 and Test 7; and of Test 1 and Test 8. The former is represented in Figure 34. In this case it is seen that from the score on Test 1 it is very difficult, if not impossible, to determine what is the most likely score on Test 7. The regression line running through the points, and making the best possible fit with them, is nearly horizontal; and constitutes a particularly poor fit. The correlation in this case is found to be,

$$r = .07,$$

which is very close to zero.[1] The comparison of Test 1 and Test 8 is represented in Figure 35. In this case it is seen that, while the points do not fall precisely on the regression line, there is still a very good fit. It is possible to predict fairly closely what score a given pupil will have on one test, if his score on the other test is known. In this comparison the coefficient of correlation is found to be,

$$r = .98,$$

which is very close to perfect positive correlation.

In general, the relationship between pairs of measures for individuals is more likely to look like that shown in Figure 29 than like any of the limiting cases, or those closely approximating the limiting cases. In the case of Figure 29, comparing scores on Test 1 and Test 2, the coefficient of correlation is found to be,

$$r = .59.$$

Another illustration of this type would be the comparison between Test 1 and Test 9, shown in Figure 36. In this case it will be observed that the fit of the points to the regression line is not quite so good as it is in Figure 29. The correlation is therefore somewhat lower, and is found to be,

$$r = .38.$$

---

[1] The method of determining correlation is not explained, as it is beyond the scope or purpose of this discussion. The technique of computation is not absolutely necessary to an understanding of the concept of correlation, and the nature of the relationship represented by various degrees of correlation.

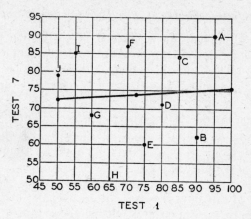

Figure 34. A close approach to perfect zero correlation.

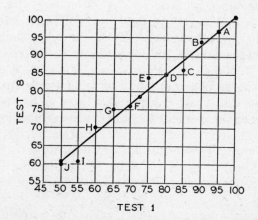

Figure 35. A close approach to perfect positive correlation.

The Correlation Table

In actual practice, the coefficient of correlation may be found without setting up a graphical representation, or correlation table, as has been done in these examples. Whenever there are only a few data, or a few cases, or a few individuals involved in the comparison, some method of computation based on the scores themselves and without constructing the graph, may be used. But as soon as the number of cases becomes large, such direct computation becomes exceedingly tedious.

In such a case it is common practice to make use of the procedure of grouping the data into convenient class intervals, on both measures, and putting them into a sort of combined graph and table, as in Table XIII. In this case, the data on one measurement have been indicated on the vertical axis in class intervals of 10, and the data of the other measurement have been indicated on the horizontal axis in class intervals of 5. Thus, an individual who had a score of 84 on one measure and 42 on the other would fall in the space between 80 and 90 on the vertical axis, and between 40 and 45 on the horizontal. He is, therefore, represented by placing one tally in the cell bounded and located by the lines 80 and 90 in the vertical direction, and the lines 40 and 45 in the horizontal. This type of arrangement is known as a *correlation table,* and may frequently be seen in statistical presentations. From this table itself, by means of the correct procedures, it is possible to obtain a very close approximation to the coefficient of correlation. It will, however, be only an approximation, since the identity of the individual cases has been lost by placing them in class intervals, or cells. But if enough cases are involved, the result so obtained will be almost precisely the same as that found by using the exact values of scores for each individual.

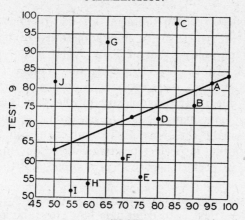

TEST 1

Figure 36. Correlation here is somewhat lower than that in Figure 29.

TABLE XIII

A Typical Correlation Table

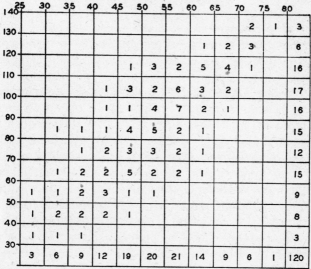

	25	30	35	40	45	50	55	60	65	70	75	80	
140													
130										2	1		3
120								1	2	3			6
110					1	3	2	5	4	1			16
100				1	3	2	6	3	2				17
90				1	1	4	7	2	1				16
80		1	1	1	4	5	2	1					15
70			1	2	3	3	2	1					12
60		1	2	2	5	2	2	1					15
50	1	1	2	3	1	1							9
40	1	2	2	2	1								8
30	1	1	1										3
	3	6	9	12	19	20	21	14	9	6	1		120

r = .78

In actual correlation problems in educational and social statistics, one will usually find a quantity of data more nearly comparable to that of Table XIII than to the comparisons in Table XII. However, the simpler examples, based on few cases, were introduced first in order to avoid confusion due to the complexity of the data themselves. No matter how many data are involved, the underlying concepts will be the same. Consistent change in the same direction results in perfect positive correlation; in opposite directions, in perfect negative correlation; and the lack of any relationship whatever gives zero correlation. In most actual cases none of these limiting situations will prevail. The problem then is to determine how close the agreement is — or how closely the data fit the regression line. The result may range anywhere between 1.00 and –1.00, that is, from perfect positive, through zero, down to perfect negative correlation.

Chapter X

MORE ABOUT CORRELATION AND REGRESSION

In the preceding chapter the concept of correlation was introduced, and by means of graphs the degree of relationship which is present in perfect positive, perfect negative, and zero correlation was represented. As was pointed out, such limiting relationships are seldom encountered in actual data, and the problem of the reader is to interpret what is meant by various levels or amounts or degrees of correlation. In order to make this clear, the five correlation charts of Figure 37 are presented. In each case it will be observed that the frequency distribution, on both the horizontal and the vertical axis, is the same. The only difference between the charts, therefore, is in the way in which various individual cases are distributed in the cells — in other words, in the degree of the relationship.

The Two Lines of Regression

Brief mention was also made previously of the *line of regression* which was drawn in each of the charts of the preceding chapter; and it was defined as the line which gave the best predicted value of the measure represented on the vertical, or Y-axis, for each score on the horizontal, or X-axis. In Figure 37 it will be noted that there are two lines drawn in each correlation chart. The line A–B in each case gives the best predicted value of Y (the vertical axis) for each score on the X-axis (horizontal); while the line

C–D in each chart gives the best predicted value of X (horizontal axis) for each score on the Y-axis (vertical).

Illustrations and Interpretation of Various Degrees of Correlation

It will be observed that the higher the degree of correlation, the smaller the angle between these two regression lines, and the closer they come to coinciding. In the case of perfect correlation, the two lines merge into one, and there is only one regression line. In such a case there is, of course, perfect prediction. If one knows that perfect correlation exists, and knows the score for a particular individual on one measure (test, scale, or whatever it may be), he can predict precisely what the score for that individual on the other measure will be. As the correlation decreases, the accuracy of prediction also decreases. Thus, in Figure 37-*A*, with correlation of .90, it is seen that the two regression lines almost coincide, and for most of the table a prediction of the score on one measure based on a knowledge of the other would be very close to the actual score.

In Figure 37-*B*, where the correlation is .70, it is observed that the individual cases have spread out somewhat from the fairly compact form they show with a higher correlation. In this case the two regression lines have drawn farther apart, and consequently a prediction of the score on one axis from a known score on the other would stand somewhat less chance of being precise. In Figure 37-*C* the correlation is only .50; the individual cases are even more scattered; the regression lines are still farther apart, and a prediction would have even less value. In Figure 37-*D*, with correlation of .30, a still greater spread of the cases and a still greater divergence of the regression lines can be observed. In Figure 37-*E* the correlation is very close to zero — just .10.

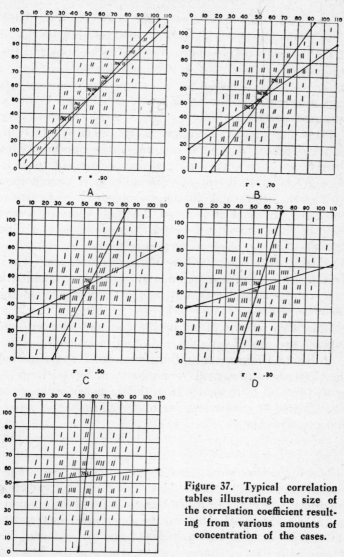

Figure 37. Typical correlation tables illustrating the size of the correlation coefficient resulting from various amounts of concentration of the cases.

The cases are scattered almost at random over the table (restricted only by the fact that there are very few cases at the extremes of the distribution on each axis), and the regression lines are almost perpendicular to each other. In this case, prediction of the score represented on one axis from the score on the other would be, for all practical purposes, worthless.

These five graphs of Figure 37 are intended merely to give the reader a general picture of the appearance of correlation charts representing various degrees of relationship. When a coefficient of correlation is presented in a research report, it usually is not accompanied by the correlation chart on which it is based. The inexperienced reader may sometimes be misled by the discussion into assuming a much closer agreement between the two sets of scores than is actually warranted by the correlation table itself. This does not mean that a correlation must always approach 1.00, or .90, in order that it may indicate a valuable or significant degree of relationship. As a matter of fact, frequently a correlation of .40 or .50, and sometimes of less, between two sets of variables, indicates a relationship which is of the utmost importance. But if the reader keeps in mind the charts here presented — or uses them for reference — he will be able to recognize from the coefficient itself about what degree of compactness or of spreading of the data is actually represented.

Non-Linear Correlation

The discussion of correlation so far presented has assumed certain restrictions which lead to the simplest correlation situations. For example, it has been assumed in the examples given that the relationship can be determined in terms of the degree of fit of the individual items to a straight line of regression. It sometimes happens that the two items of information which are to be correlated are related by some mathematical law which does not readily fit the straight (or linear) line of regression which has been used in these previous examples. For instance, a hypothetical set of data showing the relationship between years of service and salary of teachers in a particular community has been tabulated in Table XIV. Since salary schedules in general give increases in at least the early years for additional years of service, it is to be expected that this part of the table will approach a straight-line relationship. Since, however, these

TABLE XIV

An Illustration of Non-Linear Correlation

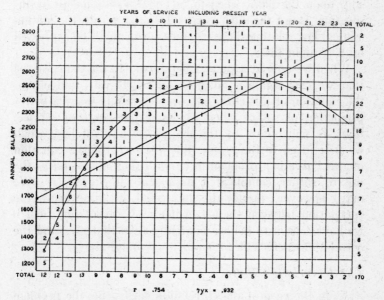

$r = .754$ $\eta yx = .932$

years of service beyond a certain point will not bring proportionately larger salaries. Variations between teachers increases do not ordinarily continue indefinitely, additional with the same period of service will, presumably, be due to such factors as difference in amount of preparation, length of previous service for which credit is given, additional duties, etc.

It is obvious that the straight line which has been drawn in Table XIV, and which is the best fitting straight line on which to predict salary in terms of years of service, is really a relatively poor fit to the data as they are. The coefficient of correlation found by the usual method indicates a degree of relationship lower than we have a right to expect. In this case it is: $r = .754$. The difficulty is brought about by the fact that we have forced a straight line (or linear) relationship upon the data, when in fact such relationship, by inspection, is not the most logical. In other words, the mathematical law relating these two measures cannot be expressed by a straight line.

When we now fit a curve (non-linear) to the data, we see that we can obtain a much better fit. If we could obtain the equation of this curve, we could certainly make a better prediction of salary when we know the years of service, than we will obtain by the use of the straight line which we first fitted to the graph. The discovery of the equation of this curve is a problem in curve fitting, and requires the use of rather complicated mathematical procedures. We may, however, merely be interested in discovering the correlation between these two items of information, which we have reason to believe is greater than that given by the correlation coefficient (r) which we found above.

The Correlation Ratio

As in the case of the correlation coefficient, the problem here is one of discovering how nearly the various cases fall on the regression line, which in this case is curved instead of straight. If it should so happen that every case fell exactly on a particular curve, as in the simple example of Figure 38-*A*, then there would be perfect correlation, or a correlation of 1.00. If the cases do not group themselves so precisely on the curve, then there is less than perfect correlation, expressed by some number less than 1.00. The relationship in such an example is expressed by what is called the *correlation ratio,* to distinguish it from the correlation coefficient. This correlation ratio is represented by the Greek letter η (Eta).

Certain differences are to be noted between the coefficient of correlation, or r, and the correlation ratio, or η. In the first place, there is just one r for a particular set of data; and, as pointed out earlier in this chapter, it is determined, in a sense, by the relative slopes of the two regression lines. In the case of η, however, there are two for each table, and they must be distinguished by the subscripts. For instance, for Table XIV, the η which is obtained by determining the fit of the data to the curve which has been drawn, is called η_{yx}, which means that it is the relationship found when we are interested in predicting Y (the measure on the vertical axis — in this case the salary) in terms of X (the measure on the horizontal axis — in this case years of service). For this particular table we find that

$$\eta_{yx} = .932,$$

which indicates a noticeably higher relationship than that of the correlation coefficient, which was .754. There is also another correlation ratio for this table; namely, that which is obtained if we attempt to fit the curve which would permit us to predict the years of service (the X-axis, or horizontal axis) from the salary (the Y-axis, or vertical axis). In this case it is found that this second correlation ratio is:

$$\eta_{xy} = .798,$$

which, while larger than r, is not so large as η_{yx}.

Correlation Ratio Is Always Positive

A second difference between r and η is that the former will range from -1.00 to 1.00, whereas the latter has a range from $.00$ to 1.00 only. This is due to the fact that η measures merely the fit of the data to some curve, irrespective of the direction of that curve. Thus, in Figure 38-B, the data run from the upper left to the lower right of the chart. The correlation ratio is still 1.00, since the data fit the curve precisely. Again, consider the data of Figure 38-C, where the curve rises in the first part of the figure, and falls in the last part. Here, the relationship, from the standpoint of the correlation coefficient, is first positive and then negative. But here also the correlation ratio, η_{yx}, is found to be 1.00, since the individual cases all fall exactly on the curve.

Correlation When Measurements Are Not in Quantitative Form

A second limitation which has been accepted in all the examples of correlation so far presented is that the scores or values for the two measurements to be correlated can be obtained in numerical or quantitative terms. This, naturally, will not always be the case. It sometimes happens, for example, that one score is expressed in some such subjective terms as "Excellent, Very Good, Good, Fair, Poor," or some equivalents. This sort of non-numerical score is sometimes found for one of the measurements, and it is desired to correlate it with scores on another variable which are found in the ordinary quantitative or numerical form. Such a case is illustrated in Table XV, in which the vertical axis represents the percentile rank in high-school graduating class of certain individuals applying for college entrance. The horizontal axis represents the ratings given by the high-school principal on a certain item of a personality

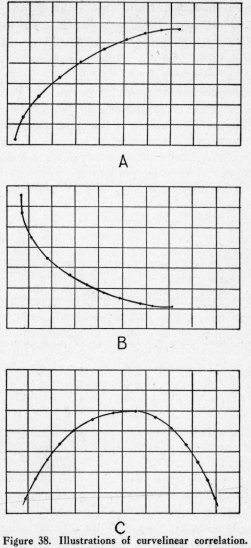

Figure 38. Illustrations of curvelinear correlation.

rating form included with the transcript of credits. Obviously, there is a relationship between the two which can be expressed by means of a coefficient of correlation. This type of table, however, requires a treatment somewhat different from that used with an ordinary correlation table in which both measures are quantitative.

TABLE XV

An Illustration of Correlation With Qualitative Data on One Axis

Distribution of a Random Selection of High-School Graduates Applying for Admission to College, on the Basis of Percentile Rank in High-School Class, and a Rating on a Personality Trait

RATING ON PERSONALITY TRAIT*

%-ile Rank H.S. Class	Aimless Trifler	Aims Just to "Get By"	Has Vaguely Formed Objectives	Directs Energies Effectively with Fairly Definite Program	Engrossed in Realizing Well-Formulated Objectives	Total
90–99				12	16	28
80–89			6	16	15	37
70–79			4	9	3	16
60–69		3	6	2		11
50–59		6	5	1		12
40–49		6	2	1		9
30–39	2	5	1			6
20–29	2	2				4
10–19	3	2				4
0– 9		1				4
Total	7	25	24	41	34	131

*In answer to the question: "Has he a program with definite purposes in terms of which he distributes his time and energy?"

Correlation When the Categories Cannot Be Ordered From Highest to Lowest

A second situation sometimes arises in which the various categories on one axis (or the subjective divisions on one of the measurements) cannot even be put in ascending or descending order as can such expressions as "Excellent, Very Good," etc. Thus, one might be interested in finding the relationship between some measurable trait on the one hand, and such a trait as political affiliation, religious affiliation, occupation, place of birth, etc., on the other. A particular individual might have in his own mind an ascending or descending scale for one of these traits, but it is unlikely that he could obtain any general agreement on that scale. Whenever one or both of the traits measured or determined for the correlation is of such character that a scale cannot be safely established, a different approach is necessary.

TABLE XVI

An Illustration of Correlation With Unordered Data on Both Axes (Coefficient of Contingency)

	Place of Birth				
Occupation	*In This City*	*In This State*	*In the United States*	*In a Foreign Country*	*Total*
Skilled Trade	178	48	35	147	408
Manual Labor	96	28	22	163	309
Semi-skilled	52	13	14	53	132
Government Service	62	5	5	13	85
Managerial	39	8	8	24	79
Commercial Service	39	8	7	14	68
Proprietor	20	7	7	23	57
Professional	15	3	3	6	27
Clerical	22	3	—	2	27
Agriculture	10	9	3	4	26
Totals	533	132	104	449	1,218

Coefficient of Contingency: C = .294

Table XVI shows such a set of data, with place of birth on one axis, and occupation on the other. The result of the measurement of relationship in this case is called the *Coefficient of Contingency,* or "C." C does not have precisely the same significance as the correlation coefficient, but it does indicate relationship in much the same way. Its one serious limitation is that its upper limit is restricted by the number of categories into which the data are divided. Thus, if there are only a few classes in each characteristic or trait, C cannot even closely approach 1.00. For instance, with four categories in each direction, C will not exceed .866. Even for nine divisions on each trait, C cannot be more than .943.

What the Coefficient of Contingency Really Measures

As a matter of fact, the coefficient of contingency really measures the amount of divergence from a perfectly balanced chance arrangement. Thus, if there are just as many cases in each cell as we have a right to expect, the C is .00. That is, if, in the data of Table XVI, the four groups as divided on the basis of place of birth each had the same proportion of its members in each occupation, there would be no relationship, and C would be .00. Since, however, the distribution differs from this exactly proportionate one, C becomes greater than zero. It is then assumed that the distribution is no longer due solely to chance, but to some tendency for one category on the one axis to be found more frequently in some one or more categories on the other axis. Thus, in Table XVI the Coefficient of Contingency is found to be:

$$C = .294.$$

This indicates a slight tendency for the various nativity groups to differ in their choice of vocations, from a purely chance arrangement. For instance, the foreign-born group are more largely represented in the manual-labor classification, in proportion to their total number, than are any of the other nativity groups.

Types of Data — Quantitative, Qualitative, Unordered

The various kinds of data indicated in this discussion are distinguished by certain names, which may help in classifying the problems involved. Whenever a particular trait may be measured by a score in numerical form, from low to high, it is called *quantitative*. Whenever it is measured by a subjective judgment, but may still be put in order from the poorest to the best, it is called *qualitative*. Whenever it can be distinguished so that the individuals can be put into various categories, or classes, or groups, but there is no safe way in which to rank them from lowest to highest, it is called *unordered*. Obviously, there can be found correlation situations in which any of these three types of measures are found in combination.

The following are illustrations of the various possible correlation situations which arise through the combination of these three types of measurements. It is obvious that either one of the two items of information which we have about each individual unit, and between which we wish to obtain the correlation, can be any one of the three kinds of measures: quantitative, qualitative, or unordered.

Nature of the First Item of Information	Nature of the Second Item of Information

1. *Quantitative*
   Score on an arithmetic test
	Quantitative
	   Score on a reading test

2. *Quantitative*
   Score on an arithmetic test
	Qualitative
	   Report card grade in arithmetic — A, B, C, etc.

3. *Quantitative*
   Score on a psychological examination
	Unordered
	   Occupation of father

NATURE OF THE FIRST ITEM OF INFORMATION	NATURE OF THE SECOND ITEM OF INFORMATION
4. *Qualitative* Rating on a health scale	*Qualitative* Rating by teachers on co-operativeness
5. *Qualitative* Rating by principal on probable success in college	*Unordered* Place of birth of parents
6. *Unordered* Occupation	*Unordered* Place of birth

Bi-serial Correlation

Certain specialized cases of correlation sometimes appear, with even greater restriction on the categories or classes than indicated in the foregoing discussion. For instance, it sometimes occurs that there will be but two categories on one axis, either qualitative or unordered. An example of the first type might arise if one were interested in determining the relationship between cloudy and bright days and some measurement of pupil performance. Days would then be divided into cloudy and bright, on some qualitative basis, involving some determination of how much sunlight there must be for a day to be considered bright. At the same time, pupils would be measured on some quantitative scale of accomplishment, say in spelling, or in addition, and the average score determined. The individual cases would then be the days, and for each day there would be a determination of whether it was cloudy or bright, and the average score of the pupils made on that day.

An example of two unordered categories would be the division of individuals by sex, and the determination of some other measurement for each. Such a correlation situation is presented in Table XVII, where the distribution is given by boys and girls on the basis of the number of extracurricular activities in which each participated. In such

a case, the ordinary methods of determining correlation will
not suffice. The method used differs so greatly that the
result is given a different name — it is called *bi-serial*

TABLE XVII

An Illustration of Bi-Serial Correlation
Distribution of Boys and Girls in a Particular High School,
in Terms of Participation in Extra-
curricular Activities

No. of Activities Participated in During School Year	Boys	Girls	Total
8	1	—	1
7	2	—	2
6	5	2	7
5	7	2	9
4	11	6	17
3	24	21	45
2	66	57	123
1	124	98	222
0	148	177	325
Total	388	363	751

Bi-serial Correlation: $r_{bis} = .143$

correlation. In the illustration of Table XVII, the bi-serial
correlation is found to be:

$$r_{bis} = .143.$$

Tetrachoric Correlation

A still further restriction is imposed if the data are found
in such a way that there are just two categories on each
axis, so that the complete table becomes a fourfold division.
Such a case may arise when there are just the two divisions
found in the data themselves. But frequently this form is
also used even when there are other degrees on each measurement, but the majority of cases fall in certain divisions,
or a certain critical line may be drawn on each trait. An

TABLE XVIII
An Illustration of Tetrachoric Correlation
Distribution of Students in Freshmen Religion Courses in
a Catholic University, on the Basis of Attendance
at Catholic Elementary and High Schools

Attended Catholic Elementary School	Attended Catholic High School Less than 4 Years	4 Years	Total
8 Years	113	164	277
Less than 8 Years	191	63	254
Total	304	227	531

Tetrachoric Correlation: $r = .528$.

illustration is given in Table XVIII. The individuals
involved were freshmen in the Religion classes of a Catholic university. Since the course was required only of
Catholic students, the presumption is that they were all
Catholic. The data in the body of the table show the number
who attended a Catholic elementary school for eight years,
or less; and the number who attended a Catholic secondary
school for four years, or less. The question here is to
measure the relationship between attendance at a Catholic
elementary school, and continuation in a Catholic secondary
school. In particular, the question is whether the completion
of an eight-year elementary course predisposes the pupil
to complete his work in a Catholic secondary school. With
such a fourfold table a still different technique is required
to measure the relationship. This is called *tetrachoric
correlation*. In the present illustration it was found that

$$r = .528.$$

Chapter XI

MULTIPLE REGRESSION, MULTIPLE AND PARTIAL CORRELATION

The Regression Line and the Regression Equation

In the preceding chapter we saw something of the nature of the line of regression, and its relationship to the coefficient of correlation. We observed, also, that when there is perfect correlation there is but one regression line, which furnishes a basis for perfect prediction. That is, when the correlation is either 1.00 or −1.00, if we know the score of any individual on one of the traits involved, we can predict with perfect accuracy his score on the second trait. But if the correlation is not perfect, then the regression line will not give perfect prediction. It will, however, indicate the most likely or most probable value of the second trait for an individual with any given score on the first trait, within the limits of our knowledge of the relationship.

In the earlier discussion we merely showed the regression lines on the correlation tables for various levels of relationship. These lines as drawn on the correlation charts may be used for prediction. However, usually the line cannot be drawn accurately on the correlation chart merely by observation of the location of the individuals as determined by their scores on the two measures. Instead, it is desirable, if not entirely necessary, to determine the equation of the regression line, and then to plot the line from this equation. This equation depends upon the interrelationship of the two traits, and is found from the data by certain statistical procedures. The problem involved in the discovery and use of a regression equation for prediction is that of determining the specific equation which best represents a particular set of data.

Examples of the Regression Equation With Perfect Correlation

The nature of the problem may be illustrated by a simple example. Suppose we have a list of the wages paid to a number of employees in a given company, together with a statement of the number of hours each has worked during the pay period, as given in Table XIX. If we plotted the

TABLE XIX		
Wages of Employees, With Hours Worked		
Employee	Hours Worked	Wages
A	38	$34.20
B	41	36.90
C	8	7.20
D	44	39.60
E	40	36.00
F	36	32.40
G	15	13.50
H	20	18.00
I	42	37.80
J	45	40.50

TABLE XX		
Wages of Clerks, With Sales Above Fixed Minimum		
Clerk	Sales above Fixed Minimum	Wages
K	$100	$25
L	180	29
M	20	21
N	240	32
O	300	35
P	80	24
Q	120	26
R	200	30
S	40	22
T	260	33

information for these ten individuals on a correlation chart, putting hours worked on the horizontal axis and amount of wage on the vertical axis, we would obtain Figure 39. When this is done, it is obvious that there is a perfect relationship between hours worked and total wages. Since this is a very simple example, the ratio between hours and

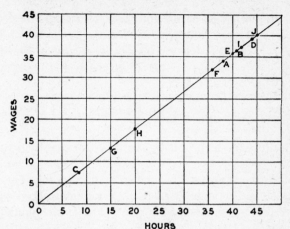

Figure 39. Perfect correlation with a single regression line
which makes possible prediction of either variable
from the other.

wages is also perfectly clear from the correlation chart
itself. It is seen that the rate of pay is 90 cents per hour.
In other words, we could now write the equation showing
the relationship as follows:

$$W = .9\,H,$$

where W stands for wages, and H stands for hours. From
either the graph or the equation it is perfectly clear that
we can predict with complete assurance the wage for any
of these workers, or for any others for whom the same
conditions hold true, if we know the number of hours each
has worked.

Usually in actual regression problems the equation is not
of this simple form because of the introduction of another
item. This point may also be illustrated by a simple example.
Suppose that the data of Table XX represent the wages
paid to a group of ten clerks in a store, and the amount
of their sales above a certain fixed minimum. When these

items are plotted on a correlation chart as in Figure 40 we discover that they also represent perfect correlation, since

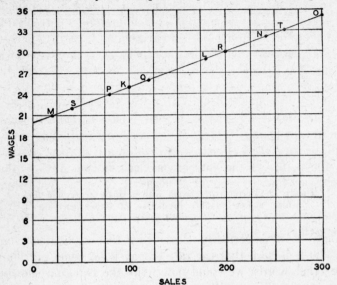

Figure 40. Another example of perfect correlation
with a single regression line.

any increase in sales (on the horizontal axis) is accompanied by a definite proportionate increase in wages (on the vertical axis). But when we now extend the line on which these points fall below the last individual on our graph, to the point of zero sales above the minimum, we find that the wages are not zero, but $20. In other words, we can write the equation of this relationship, as follows:

$$W = .05 \ S + 20,$$

where W stands for wages, and S for sales above the fixed minimum. This equation tells us that the rate of pay is fixed by the rule that each clerk receives the base pay of $20, plus a commission of 5 per cent on all sales above the fixed minimum.

In each of the above cases the equation as written may be called a regression equation, based on perfect correlation, and therefore yielding perfect prediction. In most cases of actual regression equations there will be a constant term (e.g., the 20 in the second equation above). This will be true whenever it happens that a score of zero on one of the traits or measures will not lead to the prediction of a score of zero on the other trait as well. These two illustrations are not, of course, typical of the ordinary regression problem, because the correlation in each case is perfect, and all of the points in the correlation chart fall exactly on the regression line. In such a case it is not, of course, necessary to resort to either the correlation chart or the regression equation, since the rule is easily discovered from the data themselves.

The Regression Equation With Less Than Perfect Correlation

A simple problem involving less than perfect correlation is provided by the data of Table XXI, which might represent grades earned by twenty pupils in arithmetic in one year, and in algebra in the following year. These twenty pairs of scores are represented in the correlation chart of Figure 41. When the correlation is computed, it is found to be .92. From the data it is also possible to determine the regression equation by means of which we can obtain the best estimate of a grade in algebra, for any particular grade in arithmetic. This equation is:

$$Y = .79 \ X + 14.6,$$

where Y stands for grade in algebra, and X for grade in arithmetic. Applying this equation, it is seen that the pre-

TABLE XXI

Grades of Twenty Pupils in Arithmetic and Algebra

Pupil	Grade in Arithmetic	Grade in Algebra
A	99	94
B	93	83
C	86	87
D	81	80
E	75	72
F	78	74
G	82	78
H	86	82
I	92	90
J	98	92
K	97	92
L	90	88
M	84	77
N	79	81
O	74	70
P	74	75
Q	80	80
R	84	82
S	90	84
T	96	88

diction will not be perfect. Thus, if a pupil had a grade of 80 in arithmetic, his probable grade in algebra, according to the equation, will be 77.8 (.79 x 80 + 14.6). But Pupil Q, the only one to have a grade of 80 in arithmetic, actually received a grade of 80 in algebra. Similarly, a grade of 90 in arithmetic would lead to a predicted grade in algebra of 85.7. Pupil L, with 90 in arithmetic, actually had 88 in algebra; and Pupil S, also with 90 in arithmetic, actually earned 84 in algebra.

As a matter of fact, it is seen that no one of the actual

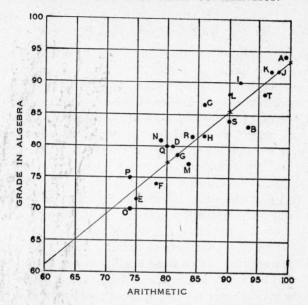

Figure 41. Less than perfect correlation showing the regression
line furnishing the best prediction of grade in algebra
when arithmetic score is known.

cases falls exactly on the regression line. However, in most
instances they do not fall very far from it. The importance
of the regression line, of course, depends on its ability to
predict the most probable grade for a pupil just beginning
his study of algebra. Any predictions so made must be
based on the assumptions that the grade in arithmetic and
the grade in algebra will continue to have the same significance as they had for the twenty individuals for whom the
original data were gathered, and that the relationship between the two measures continues to be the same. If those
assumptions are true, then it is unlikely that a prediction
would be very far from the actual grade.

The Need for the Multiple-Regression Equation

It is far too often the case that the correlation between any two measures is so much lower than the one in our last example that the prediction of one from the other by means of a regression equation is not very precise. This is due to the fact that usually most of the measures, or traits, or scores, which we would like to predict in educational and social research are so complex that they are determined only in small part by any one other measure, or trait, or score. Thus, if we wished to predict the most likely average grade which a student would earn in high school, we could obtain some information by knowing his elementary-school record. But the correlation between these two traits, in general, is far from perfect, so that the prediction would not be very accurate. If we also knew his scholastic aptitude, as revealed by a psychological examination, it is likely that we could improve our prediction if we could take that into account. If, in addition, we knew his score on rate and comprehension in reading, we might expect to find our prediction still more improved. But in order to bring our prediction to anything approaching perfect accuracy, we should also need to know something of his personality, his ambitions, his general health, and probably many other characteristics which are very difficult to measure. This process of taking into account more than one predictive factor in order to obtain a regression equation to predict some trait in which we are interested, is known as *multiple regression.*

A Simple Illustration of Multiple Regression

Suppose that we are given a list of the wages of ten clerks, and told that their sales record on three different classes of goods enter into the determination of the final wage, but that the commissions on these three classes are different. Our list of wages and sales records might look like Table XXII. When we compute the correlation between wages and each of the three items on which the total amount of wages is known to depend, we find the following:

Between wages and sales of fruit: .679
Between wages and sales of vegetables: .556
Between wages and sales on canned goods: −.263.

When the regression equations, to predict wages on the basis of each item separately, are determined, they are found to be:

$$W = \quad .039 \ F + 28.38$$
$$W = \quad .034 \ V + 28.23$$
$$W = -.016 \ C + 34.52.$$

An examination of these three regression equations indicates that no one, taken by itself, will give a very accurate prediction of the wages to be paid. In the first two, the lowest predicted wage, even if the sales of the item involved in the equation were not above the fixed minimum, the lowest wage

TABLE XXII

Wages of Clerks, With Sales Above Fixed Minimum

Clerk	Wages	Sales Above a Fixed Minimum		
		Fruit	Vegetables	Canned Goods
A	$21	$ 10	$ 10	$ 5
B	23	40	15	20
C	27	10	100	125
D	30	40	50	300
E	31	40	25	400
F	33	100	100	200
G	34	200	50	100
H	35	20	200	300
I	39	20	400	100
J	45	400	100	60

predicted would be over $28. We know, by looking at our list, that three clerks received less than this amount. The third equation gives an even less satisfactory prediction. According to that equation, if the clerk's sales of canned goods did not exceed the fixed minimum, his salary would still be $34.52; but as his sales of canned goods increased, his salary would decrease. It is obvious, then, that when there are several factors, all of which are important in determining the measure to be predicted, no one measure used alone will give an accurate prediction.

In this instance we now make use of the techniques of multiple regression. What we would like to obtain is an equation predicting wages and giving the best possible weighting to the three factors which we know are important in determining wages. In other words, we want an equation of the type:

$$W = b_1 \; F + b_2 \; V + b_3 \; C + \text{Constant},$$

where b_1, b_2, and b_3 are, respectively, the coefficients by which the sales of fruit, vegetables, and canned goods, over the minimum, are to be multiplied. The technique of multiple regression is simply the technique of discovering what these coefficients, and the constant term at the end of the equation, should be. The data necessary to discover them are all available in the original data of the problem. When these procedures are applied in this case it is found that the correct equation is:

$$W = .05 \; F + .04 \; V + .02 \; C + 20.$$

This means that the clerk is given a commission of 5 per cent on fruit, 4 per cent on vegetables, and 2 per cent on canned goods, over the fixed minimum; and these commissions are added to a basic wage of $20. When these coefficients are applied to the sales records of individual clerks, they are found to give perfect prediction. This is true because they are the only variable factors which are relevant in determining the wages paid. When they are all taken into account, in the proper proportion, the wages will be completely and accurately determined.

The Major Problem in Applying the Technique of the Multiple-Regression Equation

In the illustration just explained, once we have discovered the proper coefficients for the various factors, we can determine exactly the wage of any clerk, so long as the same conditions are maintained. Even though the original correlations, between the criterion (the measure to be predicted — in this instance, wages) and each of the individual predictive measures, are low (and in one case actually negative) it is possible to obtain eventually a perfect prediction, if we are only successful in locating all of the factors which influence this criterion. In this problem we knew at the beginning that the three factors were the only ones to be discovered. In the ordinary multiple-regression problem as it arises in educational and social research, the major question is that of determining what the important predictive factors are likely to be. And usually, even after a number of such measures have been used, and found to improve the prediction, we are still far from perfect prediction.

A Typical Multiple-Regression Problem

A typical problem would be that of predicting the average grade which will be earned by college freshmen in their first semester. For a large group of such freshmen, in the Liberal Arts College of a university, the letter grades were recorded, and changed into numerical equivalents. Thus, 4.00 would mean that the student had an average grade of A, or A in all courses; 3.00 means an average grade of B; 2.00 an average grade of C; 1.00, of D; and 0.0 would mean that he had an average of F, or had failed in all courses. The high-school records of these students were also examined, and the rank of each in his graduating class was recorded, in terms of percentiles. Thus, 90 means that the student was better than 90 per cent of his classmates, or that his average grade was exceeded by only 10 per cent. The correlation between rank in high school and average grade in first semester of freshman year was found to be .559. At the time the students entered college they had been given certain tests. One was a psychological examination, on which the average score was about 190. The correlation between this score and grade later earned was .538. They were also given an examination covering the subject matter of certain high-school courses — English, mathematics, science, and history — on which the average score was about 200. The correlation between the score on this test and college grade was .490.

Since these correlations represent far from perfect relationship, a simple regression equation, predicting college grade on the basis of any single measure, would not give very adequate prediction. By the techniques of multiple regression the three measures were all put into one equation, to predict the criterion measure, college success. This equation was found to be:

$$G = .11 \ H + .002 \ S + .004 \ P + 35,$$

where G stands for college grade, H for high-school rank, S for the score on the subject-matter test, and P the score on the psychological examination.

To use this equation to predict the grade of a freshman who has just enrolled, it is only necessary to know his scores on these three measures. Thus, for a student whose high-school rank was 90, whose score on the subject-matter test was 300, and whose score on the psychological examination was also 300, the equation becomes:

$$G = (.011)\ (90) + (.002)\ (300) + (.004)\ (300) + .35$$
$$= \quad .99 \quad + \quad .60 \quad + \quad 1.20 \quad + .35 = 3.14.$$

In other words, such a student would be expected to earn an average grade somewhat better than B (3.00). For a freshman who was at the 33rd percentile of his high-school class, and who had a score of 100 on each of the tests, the equation would be:

$$G = (.011)\ (33) + (.002)\ (100) + (.004)\ (100) + .35$$
$$= \quad .33 \quad + \quad .20 \quad + \quad .40 \quad + .35 = 1.28.$$

Such an individual would, therefore, be expected to have an average grade only slightly above D (1.00) and far below the required average of C (2.00). It could therefore be predicted with fair assurance that he would be unlikely to succeed in college.

When this equation was tried on a large number of entering freshmen, and the predicted grade compared later with the grade actually earned, it was found that for some the prediction was almost exact; some, on the other hand, were predicted either too high or too low. The average difference between the predicted grades and the actual grades later earned was about .3. This is sufficiently close to make possible some guidance, and probably would also be accurate enough to use in deciding which students should be admitted. The average difference between the predicted and the actual grades can also be foretold by means of a term called the *probable error* (explained in the following chapter) which is usually included in the complete statement of the regression equation.

Multiple Correlation

If one is interested in predicting some particular measure, he will ordinarily gather data on as large a number of likely predictive factors as he can. He will next determine the correlations between these predictive factors and the criterion (measure which he wishes to predict). He is then confronted by the problem of setting up a practicable regression equation, which will give the best return, in accuracy of prediction, for the energy involved in obtaining the measurements for those for whom he wishes to make predictions. The time and energy used in actually computing the various regression coefficients necessary to construct the equation must also be taken into consideration in deciding what factors he will use.

Naturally, the research worker would like to have some way of knowing just what predictive factors he should combine in the regression equations. Of course, he could determine the equation, and multiply the scores for all the individuals in his original data by the appropriate coefficients, thus obtaining the predicted measure. He could then correlate this predicted measure with the actual score on that measure for those individuals, and thus discover how accurate his predictive device actually is. But this would be a long and arduous process, especially if he does not know exactly which and how many predictive factors to include. He is, therefore, interested in determining what this relationship between the actual scores and the best predicted scores would be, without actually applying the coefficients to the scores of the individuals in his study.

The *multiple correlation* technique provides a method by which this question can be answered with much less effort than that required by the direct procedure just indicated. By using just the information given him by the correlation of the criterion measure with each of the predictive factors, and the intercorrelations between these factors, together with certain other statistics obtained from the data themselves, he can obtain the same effect as though he had actually tried out the various combinations for prediction. The *multiple-correlation coefficient* is written in this form: $R_{1(23)}$, or $R_{1(23456)}$, etc., which means: "The correlation between the criterion (1), and the prediction obtained by using the best weightings for the two predictive factors (2 and 3); or the five predictive factors (2, 3, 4, 5, and 6); or any other combinations." But these best weightings for the predictive factors are those found for the multiple-regression equation. Hence, the multiple-correlation technique, in a much shorter time, gives the same effect as applying the weightings of such an equation to actual cases, and correlating the result with the actual scores on the criterion measure.

In the example given for multiple regression, concerned with predicting college success, the three predictive factors correlated, individually, with the criterion of grade: .559, .538, and .490. The multiple-correlation coefficient for these factors was found to be:

$$R_{G(HPS)} = .658.$$

This means: "The correlation which would be obtained between grade earned in college (G); and the best predicted grade obtained by using the multiple-regression equation weightings for high-school rank (H), score on a psychological examination (P), and score on a subject-matter examination (S), would be .658."

In the preceding example under multiple regression, concerned with predicting wages from several factors, although the three predictive factors taken separately had correlations with the criterion of .679, .556, and −.263, when they were all taken into consideration, the prediction was perfect. Therefore, the multiple-correlation coefficient would be:

$$R_{W(FVC)} = 1.00.$$

This means: "When wages (W) are correlated with the prediction obtained by using the multiple-regression equation giving the best weightings for sales beyond the fixed minimum for fruit (F), vegetables (V), and canned goods (C), the coefficient obtained is 1.00."

Partial Correlation

The significance and value of *partial correlation* can probably be most easily explained by means of an illustration. Let us suppose, then, that we stand at the front door of a typical elementary school some time during the first week of school. Pupils are arriving on the school grounds, and as they approach the building, we call out of the groups that pass us, every third boy, until we have picked by this method a hundred boys. We now take these hundred boys into a large room in the school and record the weight of each. We then place before them an arithmetic test, on which we encourage them to put forth their best efforts; and later we score these papers. We then have two measures for each boy; his weight, and his score on an arithmetic test.

Since we have two sets of measures for the same individuals we are able to compute a coefficient of correlation. We therefore proceed to determine the correlation between weight and arithmetic score. Since by our method of selecting the boys to be measured we have probably obtained boys of varying sizes, we should obtain an interesting relationship. Our group of boys will probably include some small ones, just entering the first grade, whose knowledge of arithmetic is practically zero; and some large boys in the eighth grade who make practically perfect scores on our arithmetic test. When we compute the correlation coefficient, we discover that we have a fairly high correlation between weight and arithmetic.

If, however, we should report as a result of this test that we had found that there was a high correlation between weight, on the one hand, and knowledge of arithmetic on the other, it would immediately be called to our attention that we had overlooked one important detail. We would certainly not be entitled to expect that if we went into any room in that school, we could merely measure a boy's weight, and from that simple measurement predict with any degree of accuracy his knowledge of arithmetic. Still less, if we picked out a group of adults, would we expect to determine the score each would make on an arithmetic test merely by weighing him. Obviously, then, some extraneous factor has entered the picture to give us a measure of relationship which is not to be fully trusted.

The Effect of a Third Factor

In the simple illustration described above, it is, of course, relatively easy to discover the factor which has given us the spurious correlation. Since we picked the hundred boys more or less at random, we probably obtained a fair sampling of all grades and of all ages represented in the elementary school. It is also perfectly clear that as boys get older they will, in general, also get heavier. Likewise, as they grow older, they will tend to progress through the grades of the school, and thus be exposed to more and more arithmetic; and because of this exposure they will tend to make better scores on an arithmetic test. This factor of age is undoubtedly fairly closely related to weight, on the one hand, and knowledge of arithmetic on the other. The correlations will be by no means perfect, but they will be reasonably high.

There are two methods by means of which we can discover if there really is any correlation between weight and arithmetic score. Perhaps the simplest, in this instance, would be to obtain a large enough sample of boys all ten years of age, weigh them, and give them the arithmetic test. Or we might merely take all the fifth-grade boys, and do the same. In either case we would obtain a correlation which was not unduly influenced by the factor of extreme variation in age or in grade. If we limited ourselves to boys of the same age, we would probably find that we still had a small positive correlation between weight and arithmetic score, but this correlation would not be nearly as large as the one we found for the hundred boys selected at random. If we used boys in the same grade, we would probably find that the correlation between weight and arithmetic score was practically zero, or it might even be slightly negative — due to the presence of some dull overage boys, and some bright under-age boys in the group.

Eliminating the Effect of the Third Factor by Statistical Means

In many problems in which we are sure that our correlation coefficient is unduly large, it is not quite so simple a matter to find many cases or individuals, all at approximately the same level on a third trait. In such situations we need to make use of a statistical technique which will eliminate the effect of this third variable, without actually going to the trouble of limiting our sample to those at a single level. In the present instance we might also avail ourselves of this procedure. Thus, if we had had the fore-sight to record the age of each boy in our group of a hundred, we could apply the statistical technique known as *partial correlation*. By means of this device, and using our original sample of a hundred boys selected at random, we could still obtain a result which would be approximately the same as that found when we limited our sample to boys ten years of age, or to boys in the fifth grade. The symbol used for this partial correlation would be of the following type: $r_{12.3}$, which means "the correlation between traits 1 and 2, with 3 held constant." In this particular case, we might number our traits as follows:

1. arithmetic score,
2. weight,
3. age.

The symbol $r_{12.3}$ then means: "The correlation between arithmetic score (1), and weight (2), with age (3) held constant." This implies that we have found the same result as we would have obtained if we had selected boys all of the same age (or held the age constant by making it equal in all of the individuals studied).

This technique of partial correlation is of great value, especially in those situations in which it would be very difficult to locate enough individuals or cases, all having exactly, or approximately, the same score on the third trait, which it is desired to hold constant. Other expressions are sometimes used to describe this same procedure. For example, it is sometimes said, as in this instance, that "age has been *partialled* out," or that "the effect of age has been eliminated." Both expressions have the same significance as the one first employed, to "hold age constant." The interpretation is that the partial correlation we obtained is the correlation we would have found if all of the individuals involved were of the same age.

Holding Constant More Than One Factor

This technique is of particular importance when it is desired to "hold constant" or "partial out" more than one additional variable. For example, it is found that there is a correlation of about .60 between grade earned in high school and grade earned in college. Among those characteristics of students which are known to be related to both grades in high school and grades in college are scholastic aptitude, as revealed by a psychological examination, and knowledge of subject matter, as revealed by a subject-matter test. The question now arises: "Is there still some relationship between grades earned in high school and those earned in college, for people who have exactly the same scholastic aptitude, and have learned and retained exactly the same amount of subject matter?"

Obviously, it would be difficult to find a sufficiently large group of students who were at exactly the same level in the psychological examination and the subject-matter test, to make it worth while to compute the coefficient of correlation. However, by means of partial correlation it is possible to compute $r_{12.34}$, which means: "The correlation between (1) grade in high school, and (2) grade in college; with (3) scholastic aptitude, and (4) knowledge of subject matter both held constant." When this is done, it is found that there is still a correlation of about .20. Interpreted, this implies that whatever there is, beyond scholastic aptitude, and amount learned and retained — such as personality factors, effort, ambition, ability to influence and impress the teacher, etc. — which determine the grades a pupil will get in high school, these same factors are effective, to a slight extent, in determining his grades in college.

This technique may also be expanded to partial out, or hold constant, three factors, or four, or six, or ten, or any number which the statistician considers worth while to eliminate. The labor involved increases tremendously as each additional factor is partialled out. On the other hand, it also becomes increasingly difficult to hold them constant by selecting individuals who are at the same level on three or four or more traits. Thus, one might, in a large school system, find enough boys to make it worth while to compute a coefficient of correlation, who were of the same age, in the same grade, and had the same I.Q. (at least within a narrow range). But if one also added the requirement that they have the same reading speed, and the same score in a test of arithmetic fundamentals, it would be virtually impossible to find suitable cases. The partial correlation technique, therefore, offers the only practical method, in many instances, of determining a relationship between two measures, with the effects of a number of others held constant.

Chapter XII

MEASURES OF RELIABILITY

In the preceding chapters, we have dealt primarily with the treatment of certain specific sets of data, and with the questions which statistical techniques enable us to answer concerning those specific items of information. The problems to which we have sought an answer have been of the following types:

What is the distribution of scores on a particular test of the fifth-grade pupils in this particular school?

What is the average number of pupils per teacher in this particular school; and in a second or third particular school?

How are the scores of these two groups of pupils dispersed, or scattered, about the central tendency, that is, do we find that in one group most individuals have scores close to the average, while in another most pupils are either much above or much below the average?

How may the scores of this group of students on these two tests, with widely different possible scores, be made comparable?

How may the facts that we have discovered be made more clear by graphical representation?

What is the relationship, in terms of the coefficient of correlation, between these two measurable items, for the individuals for whom we have data?

In other words, the techniques so far described have been concerned with answering questions about certain particular limited groups of individuals for whom we have secured data with no attempt to apply or project our conclusions to other and larger groups for whom we do not have direct information.

Extending the Conclusions to Larger Groups

We come now to what is probably the most important contribution of statistics — the problem of just how much we may say with confidence about larger groups of individuals, in the light of what we know about the small sample with which we have had immediate contact. For example, if we should like to know something about the accomplishment of all fifth-grade pupils in a particular large city, it would be of immense value to us to know that we could sample that accomplishment in, say, fifty such pupils, and then arrive with some degree of assurance at some conclusion concerning the likely accomplishment of the entire group. At least, we should like to know how reliable our results, based on the small group of fifty, would be if we used them to describe the total group.

As another example, if the principal of a school becomes interested in some new teaching technique which has come to his attention, we should like to have some way of determining just how effective that technique might be, without immediately trying it out on all pupils in the school system. Or, again, if the purchasing agent would like to discover which is the most efficient of several types of floor cleaner, or of several brands of chalk, or of several kinds of paper towels, it would be a great convenience if he could try out the various kinds in one school, or in a few rooms, and arrive at some sort of conclusion about the probable result if they were adopted on a large scale. In these examples, if we found the new teaching technique superior to the old, or found one product superior to others, in the case of the limited situations in which we tried them, we should like to know how reliable or significant this result might be in determining the probable superiority of the teaching method or the product when used on a larger scale.

Statisticians have long been aware of the desirability of obtaining answers to these larger problems, and have devised many techniques designed to give, from a sample, an answer which may be extended, with some assurance, to the total group. As a class these techniques are known as *measures of reliability,* and as *measures of significance.* The use of these measures in a particular problem sometimes requires the application of long and arduous statistical computations. Their discovery, and the proof of their usefulness, usually implies the application of higher levels of mathematics. But there seems to be no reason why one should not be able to understand the general nature of the problem, and of the answers, even if he has not mastered higher mathematics, and is unskilled in the computation of statistics.

We will first discuss measures of reliability, and later consider measures of significance. Before describing any of these concepts related to reliability and significance, it is desirable, if not entirely necessary, to make clear certain distinctions and to furnish certain definitions.

Sample and Population

In the first place, the statistician usually looks upon the specific group of individuals (persons, objects, or any other entities) for whom he has obtained data as simply a sample of a larger population of similar individuals. Thus, if fifty fifth-grade pupils selected at random from several schools in a large city are measured on a given test, that group of pupils is thought of as being merely a sample of the total population made up of all fifth-grade pupils in the city; or in the state, or the nation. If one tries out, under experimental conditions, a dozen boxes of chalk of a certain brand, that dozen boxes is thought of as being merely a sample of the total population of boxes of chalk of that brand. If one determines the correlation between grades earned in high school and grades earned in college by a group of one-hundred college freshmen, those one-hundred students are considered as being a sample of all the freshmen entering that college in that year, or in succeeding years. In any case, the sample is the small number of individuals, or things, which have been measured; the population is the total group of similar individuals, or things, of which this small group is thought to be reasonably typical.

Statistic and Parameter

When some one statistical procedure has been applied to the data obtained for the particular group under observation, the result is known as a *statistic*. Thus, if the mean score earned by one group of fifth-grade pupils is found, that mean score is a statistic. If the standard deviation, or sigma, of the group of data is found, that is also a statistic. If the correlation is found between the scores of this same group of individuals on two tests or other measurements, that coefficient of correlation is also a statistic. Now, since this group is merely a sample of the larger total population, there must also be a mean, a sigma, and a coefficient of correlation which would be found if data had been gathered for the entire group. This mean, or sigma, or coefficient of correlation for the total population is known as the *parameter*.

In most cases, the parameter for the total population is never actually found, because of the great difficulty and expense in time and money involved in measuring all individuals included in the total population. An exception might be the regular decennial census of the United States, in which no time or money is spared in the attempt to reach the entire population. Thus, the mean age as reported by the 1940 census will approach very close to being a true parameter, and not simply a statistic. However, if one simply selected a thousand citizens at random throughout the country, and from them obtained the same information, the average age derived from such a set of data would be a statistic.

The principal problem involved in this notion of reliability and significance is that of determining something about the parameter of the total population, on the basis of the information given by the statistic of the sample. Naturally, if one has not obtained data for the total population, he will not be able to say with certainty what a particular parameter will be. However, if he has observed certain precautions, he may be able to make certain rather definite statements about what the parameter may or may not be. Thus, from the mean (statistic) of a sample, he may be able to conclude that the mean (parameter) of the total population must fall within certain limits — cannot be larger than some given number, or smaller than some other given number. Or, to put it a little more precisely, he may be able to determine the probability, or chance, that a sample with a mean (statistic) of fifty might have been obtained if the total population from which the sample came actually has a mean (parameter) of sixty.

The Random Sample

The most important precaution which must be followed in order to make use of these tests of reliability and significance is that the sample from which the actual data are obtained must be a *random sample* of the population. That means that no bias of any kind entered into the choice of the members of the population who were to be included in the sample — in other words, every member of the total population must have an equal opportunity of being included in the sample. For instance, if one were going to test a dozen boxes of chalk of a certain brand, he must be sure that the boxes he selects are random, or chance, samples of the total output of that brand. Obviously, if the manufacturer should supply a dozen boxes which had been carefully selected because they were superior to the average run of the product, that would be, not a random, but a biased sample. From such a sample no conclusions of any value could be deduced concerning the general effectiveness of that brand of chalk. Similarly, if the superintendent wishes to reach certain conclusions concerning the attainments of fifth-grade pupils in his school system, but selects for his test the fifth grade in a school known to be located in a superior residential section of the city, or one known to have superior teachers, his conclusions concerning the total group will be biased and of no value, because of the bias of his sample.

Sampling Error and Sampling Distribution

When a particular limited sample (random or otherwise) has been drawn from a total population, naturally the best estimate that can be made of the various parameters (mean, sigma, etc.) for the total population, from that sample alone, will be the statistics (mean, sigma, etc.) derived from the sample. Thus, if a sample of fifty cases (say, fifty fifth-grade pupils) is drawn from the total population (all fifth-grade pupils in the city) and on the particular measure used (test, rating scale, weight, height, or what not) the mean is computed, that mean (statistic) is for the moment the best estimate we can make of the mean (parameter) of the total group.

For instance, if for the sample of fifty cases, the mean

(statistic) on a particular test is 65, this furnishes an estimate of the mean (parameter) of the total population on that test, which, so far as we know, may also be 65. However, in general, the mean (parameter) of the total population will not be exactly 65. It may be 66, 67; 64, 63; or even 70 or 60 — or even some number much further removed from the mean (statistic) we have found for the sample. The difference between the mean of the total population (parameter) and the mean of the sample (statistic) is called a *sampling error*. If the error is due solely to the fact that we have made a random sample, this is called an *error in random sampling,* or, sometimes, the *experimental error*. In such a situation the error, or difference, will be due to the chance factors involved in the random selection of the cases in the sample.

If a large number of samples are drawn from the same total population, and the same statistic (e.g., mean) is computed for each of these samples, it is likely that there will be a variety of results. Thus, the next sample of fifty might yield a mean of 60, the next a mean of 68, the next of 72, etc. It would be possible, then, to make a frequency distribution of the means (or of any other statistic) found for these many samples. If it is assumed that an infinite number of such samples could be drawn, and the distribution of a single statistic (such as the mean) for all of the samples could be made, this distribution would constitute what is called the *sampling distribution* of the total population. Naturally, it would not be possible to make an infinite number of samples, and thus to determine specifically this sampling distribution. However, for many kinds of sampling situations it is possible to describe the form which this sampling distribution would take. Such a description can be shown, by means of certain mathematical procedures, to be theoretically correct, even though it can never be demonstrated by the actual selection of an infinite number of samples.

The Standard Error

The most common type of sampling distribution encountered in educational research is what is called the *normal distribution,* or the *normal frequency curve.* This is a special kind of curve, defined by a rather complicated

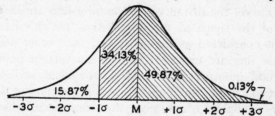

Figure 42. Typical normal frequency distribution showing sigma divisions of the base line.

formula, which has been shown to describe the manner in which results will distribute themselves if they depend on pure chance. When the sampling distribution has been constructed, or more precisely, when its form and nature have been determined by means of mathematical techniques, it is, of course, possible to treat it like any other distribution. Thus, the sampling distribution will also have a mean and a standard deviation. The standard deviation of such a sampling distribution is known by a special name; it is called the *standard error* of the particular statistic. Thus, if it is a sampling distribution of the means of an infinite number of samples, we can determine the standard error of the mean (the standard deviation of the distribution of the means of this infinite number of samples).

A typical normal frequency curve is shown in Figure 42. Since the shape of this curve is defined by means of a formula, it is also possible to know many things about it. Thus, both the mean and the median of the distribution represented by this curve will be at the point at which the curve is highest. Also, the curve is completely symmetrical about the mean or median. In addition, since the equation of the curve is known, it is possible by means of a mathematical procedure to determine exactly the area under the curve from the center or mean to any other point — or between any two points. Ordinarily, to facilitate use of the curve, the distances on the base line are defined in terms of the sigma of the distribution. On this basis, the mean is considered as falling at zero, and other points on the base line are expressed as being a certain number of sigma units above (to the right of) the mean, or below (to the left of) the mean. Tables have been computed and are readily available which give the area under the curve between the mean (or zero point on the base line) and the point (in either direction) defined by the distance 1 sigma, 2 sigmas, or any other value of sigma.

Determining the Probability of a Given Occurrence

In order further to facilitate the use of the tables, the total area under the curve is given the value 1.00, so that the area reported for a given segment of the curve is in decimal form, and may be immediately translated into a per cent of the total distribution. Thus, if the area from the mean to a certain point is reported as .40, it is readily seen that that segment of the curve is equal to 40 per cent of the total area. The total area from the mean to the end of the curve in one direction will, naturally, be .50, or 50 per cent of the total area of the entire curve. Therefore, from this point to the end of the curve the area remaining will be 50 per cent minus 40 per cent, or 10 per cent of the total.

In Figure 42 the distance of 1 sigma is laid off to the left of the mean, and the area defined by these two points is shaded. According to the table of areas, it is found that the area from the mean to a point 1 sigma from the mean will be .3413; or, in other words, 34.13 per cent of the total area. The area of the unshaded portion to the left of 1 sigma will therefore be 50 per cent minus 34.13 per cent, or 15.87 per cent. From the mean to the point 3 sigmas above the mean, also indicated on Figure 42, the area will be, according to the table, .4987, or 49.87 per cent of the total. The remaining unshaded area in that direction will therefore be 50 per cent minus 49.87 per cent, or 0.13 per cent.

Now let us see the interpretation of this type of information from the sampling distribution for a specific example. Suppose, for instance, that it is known that the mean (parameter) for a certain total population on a given trait (e.g., test score) is 56, and that the mean (statistic) determined for a particular sample drawn from that population is 60. Suppose, further, that it is found that the sigma of the sampling distribution for this mean is 2 (this will be the standard error of that mean). The mean of the sample is therefore 4 points, or 2 sigmas, above the mean for the total population. By looking in the table which gives the area under the curve from the mean to each sigma distance from the mean it is found that the area under the normal curve from the mean to a point 2 sigmas from the mean is .4772, or 47.72 per cent of the total area. Thus, beyond that point, in the same direction, there will remain an area of only 50 per cent minus 47.72 per cent, or 2.28 per cent of the total area. But the sampling distribution in this case is merely the distribution of the means of a large number of samples taken from this total population for which the mean (parameter) is known to be 56. It therefore appears that among this large number of samples only 2.28 per cent of them will be found to have a mean as large as 60, or 4 points, or 2 sigmas above the mean of the total population. Since the normal curve indicates the distribution due to chance, this result furnishes a measure of the probability that such a sample could have been drawn purely at random from the total population. That is, there are 2.28 chances out of 100 that a sample with a mean of 60 could have been selected, purely by chance, out of a total population whose mean is 56.

Determining the Limits Within Which a Parameter Will Probably Be Found

The more usual situation, of course, is one in which we know only the statistic (mean, in this instance) of the sample, and not the parameter (mean) of the total population. The operation is then somewhat different, but the conclusion must be interpreted in much the same way. Frequently in educational and social research a particular statistic will be reported, followed by its *standard error* (the standard deviation, or sigma, of the sampling distribution). Thus, if the above mean were reported as 60, with a standard error of 2, the reasoning would be somewhat as follows. The area from the mean of the normal curve to 1 sigma above is .3413, or 34.13 per cent of the total distribution. The area of the tail of the distribution, in the same direction, is 50 per cent minus this 34.13 per cent, or 15.87 per cent of the total. Therefore, if the true mean of the total population (parameter) were 58, so that our sample mean (statistic) is 2 points, or 1 sigma, more, our sample would be one whose mean fell in this tail of the sampling distribution. In other words, in only 15.87 per cent of all of the samples drawn from the total population would the mean be as large as, or larger than, the mean of this particular sample. Similarly, if the true mean (parameter) of the total population were 62, so that the mean (statistic) of our sample were 2 points, or 1 sigma, less than the true mean, our sample would have a mean which fell in the tail of the distribution to the left of 1 sigma below the true mean.

By inverse argument, then, it is often said that the probability is 68.26 out of a 100 that the true mean (parameter) of the total population will be found to be between 1 standard error below and 1 standard error above our sample mean (statistic). This is arrived at by adding the probability of 34.13 out of a 100 that the sample mean will not be more than 1 standard error above the true mean, to the similar probability that it will not be more than 1 standard error below the true mean. In other words, the probability is 68.26 out of a 100, or about 2 to 1, that the true mean (parameter) of the total population from which our sample is drawn will be between 58 and 62. Similarly, it is found by reference to the table that the area of the sampling distribution from the mean to a point 2 sigmas from the mean is .4772. By the same reasoning, it follows that the probability is twice this, or 95.44 out of 100, that the true mean (parameter) will lie within the area between 2 sigmas below and 2 sigmas above; in other words, that it will fall between 56 and 64. In the same way it is found that the probability that the true mean will be found between 54 and 66 (3 sigmas below and 3 sigmas above the sample mean) is 99.74 out of a 100.

The Probable Error

Even more common in educational and social research is the use of the *probable error*. This is a concept very similar to the standard error. In Figure 43 is shown another normal frequency curve, on which the probable error has been shown as a distance on the base line. The popularity of this measure of reliability is probably due to the

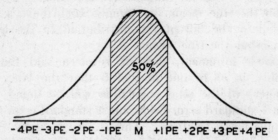

Figure 43. Typical normal frequency distribution showing probable error divisions on the base line.

simplicity of the interpretation. The probable error of a statistic is simply the quartile deviation, or Q of the sampling distribution of that statistic. Thus the area under the curve of the sampling distribution, from the mean to a point 1 P.E. (one probable error) above the mean, is exactly .25, or 25 per cent, or one-fourth of the total area. From this it follows that the area between 1 P.E. below the mean and 1 P.E. above the mean is twice 25 per cent, or exactly one-half of the sampling distribution.

The customary manner of writing a statistic to show the probable error may be illustrated by the following:

$$\text{The mean is } 56.0 \pm 2.0.$$

This is read: 56 plus or minus 2. This indicates that the mean (statistic) for the particular sample involved was found to be 56; and that the probable error of that mean is 2.0. In other words, by the inverse reasoning used above, it is said that the chances are even, or 50 out of a 100, that the true mean (parameter) will be between 54 (1 P.E. below) and 58 (1 P.E. above). In the same way, the area under the sampling distribution (normal frequency curve) from the mean to 2 P.E.'s above the mean is 41.13 per cent of the total area. It is therefore concluded that the probability is twice this amount, or 82.26 out of a 100, that the true mean will be found between 52 and 60 (2 P.E.'s, or 4 points below, to 2 P.E.'s, or 4 points above, our sample mean). Similarly, the probability that the true mean falls between ± 3 P.E.'s, or between 50 and 62, is 96.70 out of a 100; and the probability that it will fall between ± 4 P.E.'s, or between 48 and 62, is 99.30 out of a 100.

The Use of Measures of Reliability

While in the examples used above, the notion of standard error and probable error were applied to the mean, these measures of reliability may also be found for any other statistics. Thus, there will also be a probable error of sigma; a probable error for a percentage frequency, a probable error of the median, of the first quartile, or of any percentile, etc.; and a standard error for each as well. In each case the interpretation is much the same as that given above. The probable error of any statistic gives us some idea of how much reliance we may place on such a measure, as representing the total population from which the sample was drawn. If the probable error is large in proportion to the statistic computed, then we see that it does not give us a very safe estimate. Thus, if it is reported that sigma for a particular sample is 20 ± 5, we see that the chances are even that the sigma for the total population of which this is a sample may be anything from 15 to 25; and there is some possibility that it may be as small as 10 or as large as 30.

If, on the other hand, the probable error is small in proportion to the statistic, this may be interpreted to mean that the statistic probably furnishes a fairly reliable indication of the parameter for the total population. Thus, if a correlation coefficient for a particular sample is reported as .60 ± .02 we know that the chances are even that the correlation for the total population will not be less than .58 or more than .62; and the chances are very remote that it might be as small as .52 or as large as .68.

Chapter XIII

MEASURES OF SIGNIFICANCE
(Significance of Differences)

Very closely related to the problem of reliability as discussed in the preceding chapter is that of significance. The same general concepts of sample and population, of statistic and parameter, of sampling error and sampling distribution, must be kept in mind. In the case of some of the measures of significance, the sampling distribution will be the normal frequency curve, but in other instances certain other types of distributions have been found to give a more acceptable interpretation. In general the question that is answered by these measures is whether some statistic which has been found for a sample out of a general population is *significant* or *statistically significant*. The meaning of these terms will be made clear as the discussion proceeds.

The Probable Error of the Difference Between Two Means

We shall begin with a measure of significance which is simply an application of the concept of standard error and probable error. While we shall limit the discussion to the probable error of the difference between two means, it is to be understood that an analogous situation holds true for the standard error of such a difference, and also for either the standard error or the probable error of the difference between other statistics, such as percentages, or sigmas, or coefficients of correlation.

Typical Problems

The problem which is answered by the consideration of the probable error of the difference between two means may be illustrated by situations like the following:

1. In a university testing program we have given a mathematics test to all entering freshmen. When the results are tabulated by colleges in the university we find, of course, a great deal of overlapping of scores between students enrolled in the various colleges. But we find also that the average score for freshmen in the College of Engineering is appreciably higher than that for freshmen in Liberal Arts, or in Journalism. We now ask the question: Does this signify that our sample of freshmen in Engineering really come from a distinct group of high-school graduates, with respect to knowledge of mathematics? Or could it be possible that the freshmen in the various colleges are merely random samples of the total population of high-school graduates. In other words, may the difference that we have noted be due entirely to chance?

2. From a questionnaire study we obtain data on the number of years of training beyond high school for the elementary-school teachers in a number of cities. We tabulate in one list those teachers who are in cities which have a single-salary schedule, and in another those in cities which pay their elementary and high-school teachers on different scales. We note, of course, that there is a considerable overlapping between the two distributions — some teachers in each group have less than two years of training, many have two years, many have three years, and some have four or more years of training. But we also discover that the average for our group from the single-salary cities is higher than that from the group with the position type schedules. We should now like to know whether this result

implies that these samples we have drawn of teachers from the cities with the two types of salary schedules are really representative of these two total populations. In other words, can we safely infer that in school systems with single-salary schedules the average training of elementary-school teachers will be higher than the average in systems using the position type schedule?

3. We select two groups of pupils who are as nearly alike as possible in ability to learn, or in knowledge of arithmetic, or both. We then teach the first group some new arithmetical concepts by means of the teaching technique which we have been using in our school. The second group is taught these same concepts by means of new teaching technique which we have developed. At the end of the teaching period we administer the same test to both groups and find a somewhat higher average score for the class which has been taught by the new method. Can we then conclude immediately that this new teaching method is superior to the one we have been using previously? Or is it possible that the difference we have found is a difference which could have been found between two classes similarly matched at the beginning, and both taught by the same method? In other words, is the difference to be explained as due to chance, or is it possible that it is due to the difference in teaching technique?

Interpreting the Results to Discover If There Is Statistical Significance

To illustrate the reasoning in connection with the Probable Error of the difference between two means, let us take the last illustration. Suppose it is found that the average score made by the experimental group — the one using the new teaching technique — is 86, and the average made by the other, or control group, is 80. At first glance it appears obvious that the experimental technique of teaching has produced superior results. However, it is now time to apply the test of significance, and so we compute the probable error of the difference between the means. Suppose we find that this measure, PE_{M1-M2} (the probable error of the difference between the first mean and the second mean) is 4.0.

We recognize that in this case, as in the tests of reliability, we are dealing with samples. We could presumably repeat the experiment with another pair of classes, and with a third pair of classes, and with many more such pairs of classes. If we did this we know that we would not always obtain a difference of six points between the mean scores earned by the two groups. In some instances the difference might be more than six points, and in other instances it might be less than six points. In other words, just from using the two classes which we had in our experiment, we cannot say with any degree of confidence that the new teaching technique will always produce an average score six points higher than would have been obtained by the use of the other teaching method. We do not need to be too much concerned with what the average difference would actually be if we used many pairs of classes and made a distribution of the differences in means between the pairs. We are, however, very much concerned with the question of whether this actual mean difference might be zero, or might even show an advantage for the other group — in other words, be less than zero. We see, therefore, that the problem reduces to one involving the same type of reasoning as that used in our previous consideration of other probable error situations.

In the illustration here being employed, we have noted that the difference between the means is 6.0 points, which may be thought of as falling somewhere on the base line of the normal frequency curve which represents the sampling distribution (the distribution of a large number of differences between corresponding pairs of classes similarly selected and similarly treated). This situation is represented in Figure 44. We have also discovered that the probable error

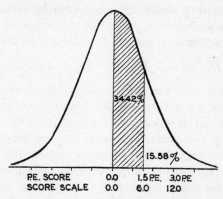

34.42%

15.58%

| P.E. SCORE | 0.0 | 1.5 P.E. | 3.0 P.E. |
| SCORE SCALE | 0.0 | 6.0 | 12.0 |

Figure 44. Typical normal frequency distribution indicating the score scale and the equivalent P.E. score.

of the difference between the means, PE_{M1-M2}, is 4.0 points. In other words, the point 0.0 on the base line of this sampling distribution (normal curve) lies 1.5 P.E.'s (6.0 divided by 4.0 — the total number of points divided by the number in 1 P.E.) below the point which we discovered for our particular pair of samples. When we look in a table giving the area of the normal curve between the mean (the point 0.0 P.E.) and a point 1.5 P.E.'s away, we find that this segment of the curve includes 34.42 per cent of the total area. The remainder of the area in the tail of the curve beyond 1.5 P.E.'s is therefore 15.58 per cent of the total (50.0 per cent, or the area of that half of the curve, minus 34.42 per cent). In other words, if the true mean of this sampling distribution (the mean difference between the means of a large number of pairs of similar classes) were zero, the chances of finding a difference as large as the one we found in this instance would be 15.58 out of 100. We are likely to conclude that something which could have happened, by chance alone, 15.58 times out of a 100, might very easily have occurred by chance in this instance. We therefore say that the difference of 6.0 points between these means is not *statistically significant*.

A Smaller Difference May Be More Significant

Let us now examine the results of another experiment in which we try out two different teaching methods on two matched groups. In this instance we find that for the experimental group the average score is 95, and for the control group the average is 90. In other words, the difference between these two means is 5.0. We might now conclude that since this difference is less than the one we found in the previous experiment, it therefore could not possibly be significant. However, we compute the probable error of the difference between these two means, $PE_{M_1-M_2}$, and find that it is only 1.0. This could easily be possible, since $PE_{M_1-M_2}$ is not at all dependent on the means themselves, or their difference; it is determined entirely by the number of cases involved, and the standard deviation, or the amount of dispersion, of each distribution.

We now apply the same reasoning as above, and note that if the true average of the difference between the means of a large number of similar samples were 0.0, then this difference we have found is 5.0 P.E.'s away on the base line of the normal curve. Figure 45 represents the situation found in this experiment. When we look in the table we discover that the area of the normal curve from the mean, or 0.0 P.E., to the point 5.0 P.E.'s distant is 49.96 per cent of the total area. In other words, the area of the tail of the distribution in that direction is only 0.04 per cent of the total. We interpret this to mean that out of a large number of similar pairs of classes, in only .04 instances out of a 100, or four out of 10,000, would we find a difference in the

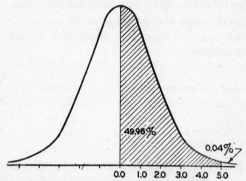

Figure 45. Typical normal frequency distribution indicating the percentage of the cases found beyond 5.0 P.E.

means which was 5.0 P.E.'s distant from the true difference of means of the total population, or from the average difference of means of this large number of pairs of samples. We are therefore safe in concluding that such a difference is exceedingly unlikely to have occurred by chance alone, and that therefore it is most improbable that the true difference between the mean scores of a large number of classes so selected and so taught by the two methods could be zero. In this experiment, we would say that the difference between the means is statistically significant, which implies that we are convinced that the true difference would never be zero.

The Critical Ratio

In research reports involving the procedure just explained, the results are often expressed in terms of the *critical ratio* (sometimes abbreviated "C.R."). The *critical ratio* is nothing more or less than the ratio between the difference we have found, and the probable error of that difference. Thus, in the first example just given, the results might be reported as follows:

	Mean		P.E.
Experimental group	86.0	±	2.95
Control group	80.0	±	2.69
Difference	6.0	±	4.00

Critical ratio = 6.0 ÷ 4.0 = *1.5*

In other words, the critical ratio is the difference of 6.0, divided by the P.E. of that difference, or 4.0; which gives 1.5. It is to be observed that the probable error of the difference between the means is not derived from the probable errors of the two means by either subtraction or by addition; the exact formula which is used need not concern us here. In the second example given above, the results might be reported in this form:

	Mean		P.E.
Experimental group	95.0	±	0.8
Control group	90.0	±	0.6
Difference	5.0	±	1.0

Critical ratio = 5.0 ÷ 1.0 = *5.0*

The general practice has been to require that the critical ratio shall be equal to or greater than 4.0 in order that one may be certain that the difference is statistically significant. This is a very strict interpretation, since the tail of the normal curve beyond 4.0 P.E's contains only .35 per cent of the total area. In other words, the requirement is that statistical significance can be reported only when the chances are no more than .35 out of a 100, or 35 out of 10,000, that the true difference is 0. One frequently reads a research report which concludes by saying something like the following: "The critical ratio is 2.8, and therefore the difference *is not* statistically significant." Or, the conclusion may be of this type: "The critical ratio is 6.9, and therefore the difference *is* statistically significant." In either of these instances the author is using the reasoning outlined above, and applying the criterion that the critical ratio must be 4.0 or more in order to insure statistical significance.

Small Sample Error Theory

We have explained in considerable detail the reasoning back of the concept of the probable error of the difference between two means (or any other statistics) and the interpretation of the critical ratio because this is the traditional measure of significance which has been applied most frequently in research reports in education and social science. However, it has one serious defect, which is that it is not a true measure unless there are a reasonably large number of cases included in each sample. The limitation is usually set at 25 cases as the absolute minimum. In educational and social research this has not, until recently, caused much concern, because it was almost always possible to find at least 25 or 30 individuals for whom data could be obtained. In other fields of research, such as biology, medicine and agriculture, the limitation has been much more important. In those fields it is frequently true that important conclusions are deduced from experiments involving only 10, or even fewer cases.

To meet the need of such a situation, a number of measures of significance have been developed, based upon sampling distributions other than the normal frequency curve. In recent years these other techniques have been gradually introduced into research reported in the education and social-science journals. There appears to be much weight to the arguments advanced by some writers that when we take a sample of even 200 pupils, all from 6 classrooms, we do not really have a random sample of 200 from the total population of pupils of that type. Instead, we have only a sample of 6 classes, taken from the total population of classes at that grade level. There are, of course, many other reasons for using the newer techniques, such as that they permit much greater flexibility in setting up experiments, and much greater accuracy in interpreting the results. They also make possible the testing of an exact hypothesis concerning the significance of our data.

There are certain terms which are used freely in research reports employing these other tests of significance. As usual with such technical terms, they fulfill an important purpose to one who understands them, by expressing a useful, and sometimes complicated, concept in a single phrase. As usual, also, they are likely to be confusing and appear unduly mysterious to the uninitiated. Some of these terms are: *degrees of freedom, the null hypothesis, levels of significance.* As we have found in the case of other technical terms used in statistics, they may be given fairly simple common-sense meanings, if we are not too much concerned with the mathematics of the situations in which they are used. We will attempt to make clear the significance of these expressions, and of the concepts which they describe, as they arise in connection with some of the more common measures of significance included in the general class of techniques known as the *small sample error theory*.

The t-Test

As we said above, in our description of the probable error of the difference between two means, that measure is limited in its usefulness because it cannot be applied when the number of cases, or individuals, in the sample is small. When the sample is small, the sampling distribution will no longer be the normal frequency curve. An analogous measure, used in situations involving small samples, is known as t, or the *t-test* of significance. This t is very similar to the critical ratio, in that it is the ratio of, on the one hand, the difference between two means; and, on the other hand, a measure of variability of the sampling distribution. This measure of variability is really a more exact estimate than is furnished by the standard error, since it takes into account the number of *degrees of freedom* (which will be explained later). For small samples it is very important to make this correction; for larger samples the difference between this measure and the standard error ordinarily used is practically negligible. This t has the added advantage, over the critical ratio, that it may be used to test not only the significance of the difference between the means of two samples, but also to determine whether the particular sample for which we have data could have been obtained by chance from a total population whose characteristics we know. In other words, we may by its use test an exact hypothesis concerning the total population from which the sample is drawn.

For example, suppose we have given a certain standardized test to ten pupils in the sixth grade, and obtained the following scores: 65, 69, 74, 76, 80, 87, 88, 91, 95. The total of these nine scores is 810, and therefore the mean score earned by our sample of ten pupils is 81. But we discover, by looking at the norms for this test, that the average score earned by a very large population of sixth-grade pupils is 75. We then ask ourselves: is it possible that these sixth-grade pupils really differ significantly from the total population of sixth-grade pupils in their knowledge of the materials of this test? Or is it possible that they could be merely a random sample of this total population? In other words, we should like to test the hypothesis that there would be a reasonable probability of drawing a sample such as this, with a mean of 81, as a random or chance sample from the total population with a mean of 75.

In this particular example, we see that the first, or numerator, term of our ratio is the difference between the mean of our sample (a statistic) and the mean of the total population (a parameter). In other words, it is 81 minus 75, or 6. The second, or denominator term of our ratio (the more precise estimate of the variability of the sampling distribution) we find, by applying the proper computational procedure, to be 9.849. The value of t is therefore 6 divided by 9.849, or .61. A t which has a value of .61 means nothing to us by itself, and so we must refer to a table which interprets various values of t in terms of the probability of finding such values, in a sample drawn from a total population whose characteristics we know. But when we attempt to use such a table, we find that we must first understand a new concept, that of *Degrees of Freedom*. (We have, of course, already used it in obtaining our estimate of the variability of the sampling distribution.)

Degrees of Freedom

The sampling distribution of t is not a normal frequency curve. In addition, we find that there is a different sampling distribution for each number of *degrees of freedom*. What this term means, in this particular example, is easily explained. We noted above that we had ten scores of which the total was 810 (and, therefore, the mean was 81). It would be possible to have a great many samples (groups of ten pupils) for which this same total could be obtained. For example, suppose we begin to set down, more or less at random, certain scores. Let us suppose that the first nine pupils of our group had made these scores: 66, 67, 75, 75, 90, 92, 83, 86, 89. We find that these nine scores total 723. But we started with the knowledge that ten scores must total 810; therefore, the tenth score is determined when the first nine have been found — it must be 810 minus 723, or 87. Or, to take another example, suppose the first nine scores we obtain are: 72, 73, 76, 80, 84, 86, 87, 87, 90, which total 735. The tenth score is again fixed for us: it must be 810 minus 735, or 75. In other words, even though there are ten scores, if we are bound by the restriction that they must total 810 (or have a mean of 81), only nine of them are free to vary at random — the tenth will then be determined by the difference between the known total and the sum of these first nine. In other words, we have here just nine *degrees of freedom*. In most instances in which the *t*-test is applied, the number of degrees of freedom will be just one less than the number of cases or individuals involved.

Interpretation of the Value of t as Found

In the present problem we therefore look in the table for *t* with nine degrees of freedom, and find that the chances of obtaining a *t* as large as the one we did find, or .61, are about 56 out of a 100. Or, more likely, we will merely find that it falls between the 50 per-cent and the 60 per-cent level. Since the sampling distribution of *t* is different for every degree of freedom, it is customary to give, in the tables most frequently used, the value of *t* for certain per-cents of occurrence, e.g., 1 per cent, 2 per cent, 5 per cent, 10 per cent, 20 per cent, 30 per cent, etc. In this instance, for example, we find that, with nine degrees of freedom, a t as large as .542 would be found in 60 per cent of random samples, and a t as large as .700 in 50 per cent of random samples. The t as large as .61 which we did find, therefore, could occur by chance alone in between 50 and 60 per cent of samples of ten cases each. We therefore conclude that our particular group of sixth-grade pupils might well be merely a random sample, and not a superior group.

The t-Test of the Difference Between Two Means

As another illustration, suppose that we have twelve pupils in one group, and in another group twelve more, each one matched or paired exactly with one in the first group, in initial knowledge of arithmetic. We now apply an experimental method of teaching to the first group, and the ordinary method to the control, or second group. At the end of the period of teaching we give a test to both groups, and then list the scores earned by the matched pairs in the two classes, as shown in Table XXIII. From this table we discover that the mean difference between these groups (or the difference between the means of the groups) is 3 points. We are, of course, as usual, interested in knowing whether this is a difference which could have occurred by chance. We shall, however, state the problem in the technical terminology that is customarily used.

The Null Hypothesis

We therefore say that we will set up the hypothesis that there is no difference between the groups, but that they might equally well have come from the same total population. We know that if we drew a large number of pairs of groups of this size from the same total population, in some cases we would get a difference in favor of the first group, in some cases in favor of the second, and in some cases a zero

TABLE XXIII

Final Scores in Arithmetic, by Matched Pairs, for Two Groups
Taught by Two Different Methods

Pair	Experimental Group	Control Group	Difference
1	92	84	8
2	84	85	−1
3	87	83	4
4	76	78	−2
5	86	79	7
6	90	88	2
7	95	89	6
8	80	79	1
9	81	82	−1
10	86	81	5
11	88	83	5
12	87	85	2
Mean	86	83	3

difference. So far as we know, the differences might be
1 point, or 2 points, or 3 or more points. But we know also
that if we drew enough such pairs of samples, and arranged
the differences in a frequency distribution, the mean
difference would be zero. In other words, the mean of our
sampling distribution of differences would be zero. The
procedure of determining the significance of the difference
in this problem is therefore reduced to that of testing the
hypothesis that the true difference of a large number of
samples is zero. This is known as the *null hypothesis* — in
other words, the hypothesis that the parameter (in this case
the difference of the means) is really zero. In testing this
hypothesis, we examine the sampling distribution to
determine the chances out of a hundred that a difference
(statistic) as large as the one we found for our pair of
samples could be found if the true difference (parameter)

were zero. Or, in other words, if such a difference could be found if these two groups were really merely random or chance samples from the same total population.

Levels of Significance

In this particular problem we apply the technique for obtaining t, and discover that our t is 3.128. We next look in our table for t, and under the proper number of degrees of freedom. We note that we have twelve cases in our problem — the difference between a matched pair being considered a single case — therefore, the number of degrees of freedom will be one less, or 11. In our table we discover that, with 11 degrees of freedom, a t as large as 3.106 will be found in only 1 per cent of random samples. This is often spoken of as the *1 per-cent level of significance*. Since the t we found is even slightly larger than this, it would be found in less than 1 per cent of samples, by chance alone. As pointed out in the discussion of the probable error of the difference between two means, the requirement that the critical ratio must be 4.00 or more in order to be sure of significance, is very strict. In a small sample error theory, it is generally held that the 1 per cent level of significance (in other words, something that would happen by chance in 1 per cent of the samples) should lead to the conclusion that the null hypothesis should be rejected. In many instances, it is even concluded that at the *5 per-cent level of significance* (something which could occur by chance in 5 per cent of the samples) we may decide that the probability is too small to account for the result on the basis of chance. In our present problem we might conclude our discussion with some such statement as the following: "We find t to be 3.128. With 11 degrees of freedom, a t of 3.106 is significant at the 1 per-cent level. Therefore, the difference found is significant below the 1 per-cent level, and the null hypothesis is rejected." In other words, we conclude that this mean of 3 points did not occur by chance alone.

Interpreting the Results

It is important to note in this example that we have ruled out only one factor, namely, chance. We cannot immediately conclude that the difference must be due to the difference in teaching procedure. We have, apparently, ruled out initial ability in arithmetic, by matching the members of our groups. But there may be other, as yet uncontrolled, factors, besides the difference in teaching method, which account for the difference. Thus the null hypothesis concerns itself with chance factors only. If we accept the null hypothesis, we conclude that the difference found could easily have occurred by chance. If we reject the null hypothesis, we merely conclude that the difference cannot reasonably be accounted for by chance — we have not proved it to be due to the experimental factor.

Chapter XIV

OTHER MEASURES OF SIGNIFICANCE

This chapter will discuss three additional measures of significance which have recently been introduced into educational and social research, and which are appearing more and more frequently in the research journals. In reading this chapter one must keep in mind what has already been said in the two previous chapters concerning the following technical terms: sample and population, statistic and parameter, sampling distribution and sampling error, degrees of freedom, the null hypothesis, levels of significance.

The Chi-square Test

In some problems involving significance we are primarily interested in the way in which our cases, or individuals, distribute themselves with respect to certain characteristics. It will be recalled that in an earlier chapter we discussed certain specialized measures of relationship, such as C, the coefficient of contingency, and tetrachoric correlation. In that discussion, we were interested in determining the strength of the relationship in those specialized cases. We might, however, be satisfied to discover merely whether or not some significant relationship, other than chance, had determined the arrangement of the individuals. Whenever this is our purpose, we make use of another technique of small sample error theory, known as "χ^2" (or sometimes spelled out: *chi-square*).

To illustrate the use of this measure we will examine a

OTHER MEASURES OF SIGNIFICANCE

very simple problem. Let us suppose that we have given a spelling test of 100 words to a particular class, as a pretest. We have set as our requirement that a pupil must spell 90 of these words correctly in order that he may be excused from the regular class work during which we propose to teach the spelling of these words. We therefore will divide our class into two groups, those who are excused (who have spelled 90 or more words correctly) and those who must report for the spelling class (who have spelled 89 or fewer words correctly). We notice, however, that there seems to be a difference between the boys and the girls of the class with respect to the proportion of each group who reach this standard, and so we make up the following table:

	89 or less	90 or more	Total
Boys	14	6	20
Girls	10	10	20
Total	24	16	40

We might, of course, determine the coefficient of contingency, or use tetrachoric correlation, in order to determine the relationship between sex and ability to meet this requirement in spelling. But we are more interested, in this instance, in testing the hypothesis that girls are really superior to boys in spelling ability. The question, of course, resolves itself to this: If boys and girls, in general, are really equal in spelling ability, would it be within the range of reasonable probability for us to obtain a distribution such as that found in our table? The null hypothesis which we wish to test is this: That there is no real difference between boys and girls in spelling ability — that the two groups could really have come, by chance, from the same total population. In testing this hypothesis, we will want to determine the percentage of times, out of a very large number of samples, in which we could obtain such a distribution as this, by chance, even if the true difference (between all boys and girls) really is zero. If that percentage is large, then we will know that this arrangement could have been obtained easily by chance, and that we have no basis on which to impute superior spelling ability to girls. On the other hand, if that percentage is low, say at the 1 per-cent level of significance, or perhaps even at the 5 per-cent level, then we are justified in rejecting our null hypothesis, and deciding that something other than chance has brought about this distribution.

Degrees of Freedom for Chi-square

We therefore proceed with the technique for finding chi-square (this technique need not concern us here) and arrive at this result for this particular problem:

$$\text{Chi-square} = 1.67.$$

When we wish to interpret this value of chi-square in terms of probabilities, or levels of significance, we find that we must take into consideration the number of degrees of freedom. The sampling distribution of chi-square is not a normal frequency distribution; and, in addition, there is a different distribution for each number of degrees of freedom. In order to determine the number of degrees of freedom involved in this particular problem, we again examine the distribution. We note that we have 40 cases, or pupils, involved. But the basic consideration here is not the number of cases, but rather the number of spaces in which they might fall. We see that there are four of these; two for girls, and two for boys. However, if we look again at our table, we find that we have several restrictions in the data themselves. Thus, there were 20 boys and 20 girls. In addition, there were 24 pupils who had 89 or fewer words spelled correctly, and 16 who had 90 or more. The form of our table involving these restrictions on freedom of the data to vary, will therefore be:

	89 or less	90 or more	Total
Boys			20
Girls			20
	—	—	—
Total	24	16	40

In determining the number of degrees of freedom which we have, we must confine ourselves to these restrictions. Suppose now that we set down a number, more or less at random, in any one of the four spaces. Let us try 8 in the lower left-hand cell — girls who spelled correctly 89 or fewer words. But as soon as we have put down that figure, we note that the restrictions begin to apply. Since there were 20 girls altogether, if 8 fall in this space, the remaining 12 must be found in the lower right-hand cell. Also, since there were 24 pupils with 89 or fewer words spelled correctly, if 8 of these are girls, the remaining 16 must be boys; so the number in the upper left-hand cell is determined. Finally, if 16 of the boys are in this space, and there are 20 altogether, there remain only 4 for the upper right-hand cell. Our new table, therefore, looks like this:

	89 or less	90 or more	Total
Boys	(16)	(4)	20
Girls	8	(12)	20
	—	—	—
Total	24	16	40

Only the one frequency could be allowed to vary; once it is determined, the other three frequencies are fixed.

Suppose we try other numbers in our table. This time, let us start with the upper right-hand cell and set down the number 2. Then the upper left-hand square must contain 20 minus 2, or 18. In the same way, the frequency in the lower right-hand space must be 16 minus 2, or 14. But this also determines the frequency in the lower left-hand cell, which must be 20 minus 14, or 6. Our table is:

	89 or less	90 or more	Total
Boys	(18)	2	20
Girls	(6)	(14)	20
Total	24	16	40

In other words, we have found that as long as we are restricted by the marginal totals, the frequency in only one of the cells is free to vary; the frequencies of the other three are then automatically fixed. Therefore, we say that we have here just one degree of freedom.

Interpreting the Chi-square

We now look in the table giving value of chi-square, and discover that with 1 degree of freedom we would find a chi-square as large as the one we did find, or 1.67, in 20 per cent of random samples from the same total population. We therefore conclude that this distribution could have been obtained by chance alone if the spelling ability of boys and girls is equal. Since it could have occurred by chance alone in 20 per cent of random samples, we must grant that we have no evidence from this set of data which would lead us to say that there is any significant difference in spelling ability between boys and girls. In other words, the two groups could represent merely chance samples taken from the same total population.

Let us also examine the distribution indicated in our second table, with 4 boys and 12 girls spelling 90 or more words correctly. In this case we find that chi-square is 6.67. Looking again in the table of values of chi-square, we discover that, with 1 degree of freedom, a chi-square as large as 6.635 could have been obtained by chance alone in only 1 per cent of random samples. If this distribution had been found experimentally, therefore, we would have arrived at a different conclusion. We would note that our chi-square of 6.67 is even larger than the one at the 1 per-cent level. We would therefore have concluded that the null hypothesis was to be rejected, and that there really was a significant difference in spelling ability, between boys and girls. We would also say that we stated this conclusion "at the 1 per-cent level of confidence"; of that the difference was signifi-cant "at the 1 per-cent level."

Analysis of Variance

Another measure of significance which has an important place in the small sample error theory is that known as *analysis of variance*. The term *variance* merely means σ^2, or the square of sigma. It will be recalled that in an earlier chapter sigma was defined as being *the root mean square of the deviations from the mean*. If one simply refrains from taking the square root as the last step in finding sigma, he will, therefore, have the *variance*. *Analysis of variance* is a procedure which enables one to test, in a single operation, a number of samples, apparently drawn from several different populations, in order to determine if they could, by chance, have come from the same total population. In applying the *t*-test, or the critical ratio with the probable error, it is necessary to use just two samples at a time, and to discover if there is a significant difference between their means. The analysis of variance enables one to deal with a number of samples at one time. If it is found that they could have come from the same total population, the null hypothesis is accepted, and it is concluded that there is no significant difference between them. If, however, the null hypothesis is rejected, it is concluded that one or more of the samples could not, by chance, have come from the same total population as the others. It is then necessary to apply the *t*-test to various pairs separately, in order to discover which ones differ significantly from each other.

For example, after having given a standardized mathematics test to all freshmen enrolling in the various colleges of a university, we find that there appears to be some difference in the mean scores on the test between students in the various colleges. In order to test the significance of this difference, a random sample of eight scores is drawn from among the freshmen in each of five colleges; Business Administration, Engineering, Journalism, Liberal Arts, and Nursing. These five samples of eight each are shown in Table XXIV (not arranged in the order given above).

TABLE XXIV

Scores Earned on a Standardized Mathematics Test by a
Sample of Eight Freshmen in Each of Five
Colleges in a University

Colleges

(1)	(2)	(3)	(4)	(5)
76	59	57	55	55
70	54	61	63	55
67	59	64	51	53
59	57	56	50	48
75	71	59	54	58
68	66	55	67	54
72	59	59	56	51
72	59	64	62	47

| Mean | 69.9 | 60.5 | 59.4 | 56.0 | 52.6 |

Mean for All Colleges: 59.7.

Two Sources of Variation

In such a situation as this, the total variance for the entire group of 40 individuals may be thought of as coming from two sources — the variances within the groups, and the variances between the groups. The technique of analysis of variance is simply that of separating these two variances, coming from the two sources, and analyzing certain relationships between them.

Reporting the Results

It is customary to set up the results of the application of the analysis as in Table XXV. The column headed "Sum of Squares" represents the source of the variation indicated by the variance. The "Sum of Squares" for the "Total" line, for example, is obtained by noting the difference between each individual score and the mean for the entire table; squaring each of these individual differences or deviations; and adding them all into one sum. The column "Mean Square," where it has been filled out, merely indicates the result when the "Sum of Squares" is divided by the appropriate number of degrees of freedom.

TABLE XXV

Form for Reporting the Analysis of Variance for
the Data of Table XXIV

Source of Variation	D.F.	Sums of Squares	Mean Square
Between Groups......	4	1344.150	336.04
Within Groups	35	818.625	23.39
Total	39	2162.775	

$$F = 336.04 \div 23.39 = 14.36$$

In Table XXV the "D.F." stand for degrees of freedom. It will be observed that for the "Between Groups" row, there are 4 degrees of freedom, just one less than the number of colleges. For the "Total" row, there are 39 degrees of freedom, just one less than the total number of cases, or freshmen. For the "Within Groups" row, the number of degrees of freedom will be the difference between these two, or 35. This can also be arrived at by noting that for each group taken separately the number of degrees of freedom will be 1 less than the number of cases, or 7. Since there are 5 such groups, the total number of degrees of freedom will be 5 times 7, or 35.

Interpreting the Results

The test given by the analysis of variance may be described simply as follows: If these five samples are really samples from the same total population, then the variance (mean square) found between groups should not differ significantly from the variance (mean square) found within the groups. We should not, of course, expect the variances to be the same, but we would expect that the variation between them could be accounted for by chance, if the samples really came from the same population. To test this, we set up the null hypothesis that there is really no significant difference between the variances (mean squares). We then find the ratio between these two mean squares. In this case, it is found to be, according to Table XXV, $336.04 \div 23.39$, or 14.36. This ratio is called "F," so that we would say, in this example, that

$$F = 336.04 \div 23.39 = 14.36.$$

It can be determined, from the sampling distribution of F, in what percentage of groups of random samples an F of a certain size could be found, by chance alone, if the samples really came from the same total population. This sampling distribution is not the normal frequency curve, and it differs for every combination of degrees of freedom. There will, therefore, be a different sampling distribution for every possible pair of numbers of Degrees of Freedom. In this particular instance, we have 5 groups of 8 each, or a total of 40; this gives us 4 degrees of freedom between groups, and 35 within groups. In another instance we might have 8 groups of 50 each, or 400 cases altogether; this would give us 7 degrees of freedom between groups, and 392 within groups. For these two problems the sampling distributions would be materially different. If in a third situation we had 12 groups of 5 cases each, we would have 11 degrees of freedom between groups and 48 within groups; the sampling distribution would again be different. Since there are so many possibilities, the tables customarily used in problems of Analysis of variance give only the F which would be found at the 5 per-cent and the 1 per-cent level of significance. That is, the table will indicate, for each combination of degrees of freedom, the F which would be found by chance in 5 per cent of a large number of such sets of samples, if they came from the same total population; and that which would be found in 1 per cent of such sets of samples.

For the present example, therefore, we look in the table of F under 4 degrees of freedom for the larger variance, and 35 degrees of freedom for the smaller variance. We find that an F as large as 2.64 would be found in 5 per cent of random groups of samples of this size; and than an F as large as 3.91 would be found in only 1 per cent of random groups of such samples. Since the F which we did find is 14.36, and thus much larger even than the one which would be found in 1 per cent of the samples, we are justified in saying that there is very slight probability of finding an F of this size, by chance alone. We therefore conclude that the null hypothesis must be rejected, and that the five samples we have could not have come, by chance, from the same total population. In other words, there is some real difference, in knowledge of mathematics, between the populations from which our samples were derived. Since this is the case, we are justified in applying the t-test to the various pairs in order to discover which ones differ significantly from the others.

The Advantages of the Analysis of Variance

In such a simple example as the one just described, the advantage of the analysis of variance is that of permitting the comparison of several sample groups at the same time, to determine whether they could have come from the same total population, or really are samples of significantly different populations. A further advantage of this technique is that it makes possible the designing of experiments in which several sources of variation may be controlled. For example, if we wish to test several different types of teaching, it will be better if we can use pupils from a number of different schools. But frequently in such a problem there will be very considerable differences in the learning results between the several schools, entirely apart from the differences in learnings under the various teaching methods. The analysis of variance enables us to take account of these variations, and to determine more precisely the probable differences in the effects of the several methods, which might otherwise be covered up by the variations between schools.

Another important advantage of the technique is that it permits one to design experiments which will answer more than one question at a time. Thus, one might be interested in testing the effectiveness of several different methods of teaching. He might also wish to test the hypothesis that the various methods were not of equal effectiveness with various ability levels of pupils — the bright, the medium, and the dull. By a properly designed experiment he could test, first, the general effectiveness of the methods. He could then test the interaction effect of these various methods upon pupils in the several ability levels. If he came to the conclusion that there was a significant difference between the methods with pupils of various types, he could then set up additional experimental conditions to test these effects more precisely. If, on the other hand, he found that there was no significant difference in this interaction effect — that between teaching methods and ability levels — he would know that it was probably not worth while to proceed with these additional experiments.

Whenever the results of these more complex experiments are presented, the form of the presentation of the data will follow the general pattern set up for our simple problem. The test of significance in each case will depend on the value of F, obtained by finding the ratio between two variances. And the meaning of the F will depend on what is found in the tabled values of the sampling distribution of F, under the proper number of degrees of freedom of the two variances involved. The interpretation will also be in terms of an answer to the question whether the F indicates or fails to indicate significance at the 5 per-cent level, or at the 1 per-cent level. The result will be either the acceptance or the rejection of the null hypothesis.

Analysis of Covariance

The *analysis of covariance*, like certain other statistical procedures explained earlier, is primarily a method of doing statistically something which, in a particular situation, would be difficult or impossible, to do experimentally. For example, we may be interested in trying out several different methods of teaching the keyboard to beginning students in typewriting. We have four classes of beginners, and we decide that we would like to determine if there is any significant difference in results between the following four procedures:

1. Teach first the keys struck with the first fingers, then those assigned to the second fingers, then the third, then the fourth.

2. Teach first the eight guide keys, then, in order, certain symmetrical sections of the keyboard, such as: r,t (third bank, first finger of left hand); u,y (third bank, first finger of right hand); v,b (lower bank, first finger of left hand); m,n (lower bank, first finger of right hand), etc.

3. Teach first the eight guide keys, then the other letters in some other order, without considering their location on the keyboard; for example: e, i, r, c, n, o, etc.

4. Do not teach the fingering at all, but from the first lesson give pupils the opportunity to write something of their own composition, finding the proper location of the keys from the keyboard itself, or from a wall chart.

At the beginning of the school year we administer to the members of our four classes a prognostic test which we have reason to believe is fairly accurate in its prediction of success in typewriting. But when we compare the scores made by the four classes, we find that they are not equal in their aptitude to learn typewriting, the mean scores of the four groups being: 87, 85, 83, 80. We now attempt to equalize the classes, by transferring pupils from one section to another so that the four groups will be as nearly equal as possible in aptitude, as measured by this prognostic test. But at this point we run up against the difficulty which so often interferes with experimentation in actual school situations. Since we did not know who would be in the classes until school started, we could not arrange the groups beforehand according to ability. Since the pupil programs are now all made out, we find it utterly impossible, because of various conflicts, to make enough changes to bring the groups to anything like equality in aptitude to learn typewriting.

The Advantage of Analysis of Covariance

At this point the value of analysis of covariance is made

clear. We cannot equalize the groups experimentally — perhaps we can do so statistically. If we knew the exact regression equation by means of which we could predict typewriting ability from the prognostic test, we could apply that equation and predict for each pupil what his final ability should be. We could then proceed with the experiment as at first planned, and then make our comparisons, for the four teaching methods, between the predicted ability and the actual final ability as revealed by tests. In that case, a method which enabled the pupils to exceed their predicted final ability would be recognized as being especially efficient; one under which the pupils did not reach their predicted final ability would show itself to be ineffective. But this process would require a considerable amount of computation, and would involve the assumption that the regression equation was equally valid for each of the four methods of teaching. The technique of analysis of covariance gives us precisely the same result as though we had gone through this process, without the necessity of computing the predicted ability in typewriting.

Reporting the Results

We therefore proceed with our experiment, assigning the four groups at random to the four methods of teaching. At the end of the year we give a series of tests, and record the net speeds. We then arrange our results as in Table XXVI. This table shows, for each pupil in each class, the score on the prognostic test and also the final average net score in words per minute. It also shows the average prognostic score and net speed for each group.

We now set up our null hypothesis. In this case it is that the four methods of teaching are equally effective — in other words, that the four samples could all have been drawn, by chance, from the same total population. To test

TABLE XXVI

Initial Scores on a Prognostic Test of Typewriting Ability,
and Final Net Speeds, for Twelve Pupils in Each of
Four Classes, Taught the Keyboard by
Four Different Methods*

Classes

A		B		C			
Prognostic Test (X)	Final Net Speed (Y)	Prognostic Test (X)	Final Net Speed (Y)	Prognostic Test (X)	Final Net Speed (Y)	Prognostic Test (X)	Final Net Speed (Y)
74	25	72	30	69	28	69	22
76	29	74	24	70	25	69	25
78	23	78	26	73	24	72	22
82	31	81	35	79	34	76	30
84	27	83	33	81	36	77	35
88	38	85	37	82	41	77	29
89	39	88	40	86	37	82	30
92	43	89	43	87	43	82	35
93	45	90	42	87	42	84	42
95	42	91	46	90	49	89	37
96	46	91	46	95	46	89	47
97	44	95	47	97	51	89	47
Means 87	36	85	37	83	38	80	33

* This is a purely hypothetical example, to illustrate the problem; the letter indications of classes cannot be associated in any way with the descriptions of teaching methods.

this hypothesis, we need to find F, as in the analysis of variance, and to determine whether, with the number of degrees of freedom involved, such an F could occur in a reasonable percentage of such sample groups, all from the same population.

Our next step is to apply to these data the procedures of analysis of covariance, and set down the results as in Table XVII. This is one form which is fairly common in

TABLE XXVII

Form for Reporting the Analysis of Covariance for
the Data of Table XXVI

Source of Variation	Sums of Squares and Products				Sums of Squares	D. F.	Mean Square
	D. F.	Σx^2	Σxy	Σy^2			
Total ...	47	3303	2902	3194	644.3	46	
Between Classes..	3	323	132	168			
Within Classes..	44	2980	2770	3026	451.2	43	10.5
For testing significance of adjusted Means					193.1	3	64.4

$$F = 64.4 \div 10.5 = 6.13$$

research reports based on this technique. The degrees of freedom in the left-hand part of the table are obtained as before: for the Total, 47, which is 1 less than the number of individuals or cases involved; for "Classes," 3, which is 1 less than the number of classes. The next three columns contain certain sums derived from the variation or deviations of the various scores from the mean of the entire group. These form the basis for the variation or variance which it is desired to test. The "x" stands for the prognostic measure, and the "y" for the final measure; in this case the average net score on the tests. "Σx^2," therefore, means the sum of the squares of these deviations from the mean, for the prognostic scores. "Σ_Y^2" denotes the same for the final scores. "Σ_{XY}" indicates that we have, for each individual involved, multiplied the deviation of the prognostic score

from the mean of such scores, by the deviation of the final
score from the mean of those scores; and then added
together all such products.

In the right-hand side of the table, the heading "Sums
of Squares" does not mean precisely what it did in the table
arranged for analysis of variance; in this case the three
preceding items in the same row are taken into account
in determining the particular "Sum of Squares." The second
column in this part of the table again indicates the number
of degrees of freedom. But this time it is found that for
each row there is one less degree of freedom. This is because
the operation involves, at least implicitly, the computation
of a regression coefficient. It is a general rule that each
statistic which is computed (or implied) removes one degree
of freedom, since it puts a further restriction on the freedom
of the measures to vary. The next step is to compute the
mean squares (variances) which are required; these are,
as before, the "Sum of Squares" divided by the degrees of
freedom for a particular row of the table.

Interpreting the Results

The final procedure is to find the ratio between the two
mean squares (variances) which are involved, to obtain F.
In this particular problem it is seen that

$$F = 64.4 \div 10.5 = 6.13.$$

Referring again to the table giving values of F, it is found
that, with 3 and 43 degrees of freedom, an F as large as 4.28
would be found in only 1 per cent of sample groups, if they
were all drawn from the same total population. Since the F
which was actually found, 6.13, is even larger than the F
at the 1 per-cent level, it is concluded that the null hypothesis must be rejected. In other words, in this illustration,
we have determined that the differences in learning which

have taken place in the four classes, taking into account the initial or prognostic score, could not have been due to chance alone. If we have eliminated all other possibilities, we may conclude that the differences are actually due to the variation in teaching techniques used. It is to be observed that in this case we need not concern ourselves about the differences in initial ability, as revealed by the prognostic test. These differences have been taken into account in the application of the techniques of analysis of covariance.

Thus we see that the analysis of covariance permits us to arrive at valid conclusions concerning the effectiveness of certain experimental conditions (in this case, the several teaching procedures) even when we find ourselves unable to arrange carefully matched groups at the beginning of the study.

INDEX

Analysis of covariance, advantages of, 175 ff.; reporting the results, 177 ff.

Analysis of variance, advantages of, 174 f.; interpreting the results, 171 ff.; two sources of variance, 170 f.; value of, 169 f.

Angle graphs, *see* Circle graphs

Area graphs, 32 ff., 39; incorrect form of, 32 f.

Arithmetic mean, *see* Mean

Average, 12 ff.; *see* Mean; Median

Average deviation, *see* Mean deviation

Bar graphs, 30 ff., 39; to compare parts of a whole, 38 f.; comparing more than two magnitudes, 40 ff., 45 ff.; incorrect form of, 30 ff.

Biased sample, 137

Bi-serial correlation, 108 f.

Central tendency, measures of 11 ff.; *see* Mean; Median

Chi-square, degrees of freedom for, 166 ff.; interpretation of, 168 f.; use of, 164 ff.

Circle graphs, 37 f., 39; comparing more than two magnitudes, 41 f., 44

Class intervals, 6 ff.

Coefficient of contingency, 105 f.

Comparable scores, *see* Percentile scores; Standard scores; T-scores

Correlation, and best predicted value, 95; bi-serial 108 f.; coefficient of contingency, 106 f.; coefficient and ratio compared, 101 f.; degrees of, 96 ff.; graphical representation of, 82 ff.; multiple, *see* Multiple correlation; non-linear, 98 ff.; perfect negative, 87 f.; perfect

positive, 84 ff.; of qualitative data, 104 f., 107 f.; of quantitative data, 107 f.; ratio, 100 ff.; symbol for coefficient of, 8; tetrachoric, 109 f.; and types of data, 107; of un-ordered data, 105 ff., 107 f.; value of, 79 f.; zero, 88 f.

Correlation table, 92 ff., 97

Criterion, 125

Critical ratio, 154

Cumulative frequency, 68 ff.

Cumulative frequency graphs, 65 f.

Cumulative percentage frequency, 68 ff.

Cumulative percentage frequency, graphs, 70 f.

Degrees of freedom, 156 ff.

Dispersion, measures of, 19 ff.; *see* Standard deviation; Quartile deviation; Mean deviation

Error in random sampling, 138

Eta (η), 101

Experimental error, 138

F, 172

Frequency distribution, 5 ff.; graphical representation of, 9 f.

Graphical representation; *see* Graphs

Graphs, advantages of, 29; for continuous data, 61 ff.; and general rules for comparison of difference in magnitude, 39; specialized types of, 52 ff.; types of, 29; *see also* Area graphs; Bar graphs; Circle graphs; Cumulative frequency graphs; Cumulative percentage frequency graphs; Map graphs; Pictorial graphs; Time graphs; Volumetric graphs

183

$$\frac{\begin{array}{r} 25 \\ 21 \end{array}}{46}$$

23.